Fundamentals of Merchandise Presentation

Fundamentals of Merchandise Presentation

Robert Colborne

ST Publications
Cincinnati, Ohio

FUNDAMENTALS OF MERCHANDISE PRESENTATION

Robert Colborne

Copyright © 1982 by The Signs of the Times Publishing Company
407 Gilbert Avenue, Cincinnati, Ohio 45202

International Standard Book Number: 0-911380-59-0
Library of Congress Catalog Card Number: 82-61469

Manufactured in the United States of America

FUNDAMENTALS OF MERCHANDISE PRESENTATION

Introduction

Visual Merchandising (VM) is a sophisticated art that has evolved into an important retailing profession. It is the keystone in the merchandising scheme. Merchandise displays generate customer traffic, establish the store's image, reinforce fashion trends, and set sales patterns. The VM designer is responsible for the manner in which all merchandise is displayed in the store. He designs window displays, institutional displays, promotional displays, in-section displays, arranges merchandise in a department and selects the racks upon which the merchandise is arranged. He also travels to markets to buy props and fixtures that will complement his displays. Since all displays must reflect the store's merchandising policies, the VM designer reports directly to the store manager or company president who keeps him informed about policy and policy changes. Companies with multiple stores have a VM designer and staff in each store. In addition to reporting to the store manager, this designer may report to a corporate VM vice president, who in turn reports to the president.

Other responsibilities of the VM designer include store maintenance, minor remodeling, producing special events, sign making, and some merchandise buying. Additionally, he keeps department heads informed about new merchandise presentation trends.

The VM designer selects the merchandise to be displayed, makes or buys the props and signs to support the display, dresses mannequins, plans the lighting, and physically installs the display. As with any business

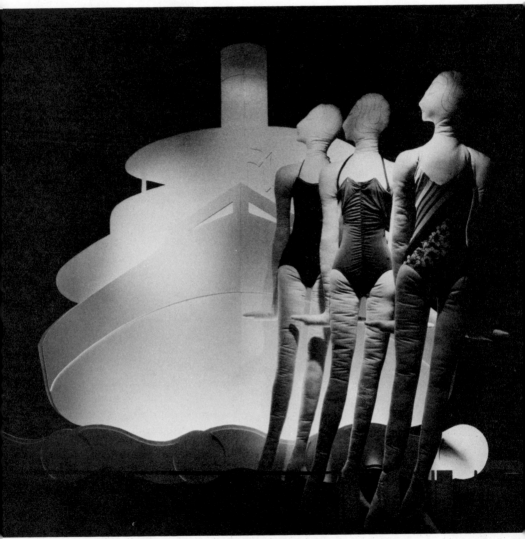

Nordstrom, Seattle WA

Woodfield Phone Center Store, Schaumberg IL

endeavor, the VM department has its share of bookkeeping. Records must be kept about the location of the merchandise and the amount of merchandise on display. Promotion and fashion schedules are prepared and maintained. The VM designer has a budget with which he pays for props, freelance artists, and the production of special events such as fashion shows. Payroll and salary budgets must be justified and supervised.

Universities and art schools offer courses to students who are preparing to enter the visual design profession. The study of design is an essential requirement for this field, so students who major in design appear to be the best qualified. Since competition is keen, a college degree is important. After all, the better you are prepared, the more qualified you are to meet the challenges of the job. Interior design majors are well suited because they understand space planning and volume design. Students will do well to take merchandising, accounting, and other business courses as a minor to complement their design major. Minor subjects should be chosen with great care, as they can become very valuable. For example, at some point in his career, the designer will be asked to manage a department or a division. He must bring into play other talents, in order to supervise employees, supply ideas, create business and art directions, and oversee budgets and acounting.

The VM designer works with all art forms: design, calligraphy, illustrations, flat pattern, volume design, space planning, sculpture, theater, model making, package design, and printing. He must understand these forms and work within their parameters to create an art expression. His art experience is less vertical than that of most commercial artists.

All art forms support a display and the display supports the merchandise. Because the merchandise changes monthly, semi-annually, and annually, and because there are a great many styles of merchandise in the store, the designer is constantly faced with changing forms. One day he may work with a dress display that demands an Art Nouveau expression and the next day he may be working with furniture that is Chippendale in design. The VM designer needs to be knowledgeable about art history, that is, to know the colors, design principles, and materials that are synonymous with each period.

The VM profession is an exciting, rewarding field that challenges your creativity from the first day on the job and every day thereafter that you pursue it as a career.

1

The Visual Merchandising Designer

Retail stores are obviously in business to make a profit by selling merchandise. To accomplish this end, the stores buy merchandise, price it for a profitable return, tell the public about the merchandise, and show it in such a manner as to make it most desirable to the public.

In the retailing scheme, the visual merchandising (VM) designer's job is to present the merchandise to the public; he determines how the merchandise is displayed in the store. Regardless of how creative the designer may be, the store's displays must meet certain criteria based upon the overall sales efforts of the retail organization. This means the visual merchandiser does not work in a vacuum, but must coordinate his activities with and understand the objectives of other departments within the company.

Large retail organizations are departmentalized, with separate units handling separate business functions. Smaller stores may have only a few departments with multiple responsibilities. It makes little difference how the responsibilities are divided, as the business functions apply to all firms. Generally speaking, large operations have the following departments with which the display director is primarily concerned: merchandising; operating; fashion merchandising; advertising; special events; accounting; personnel; and, of course, the visual merchandising department.

The merchandise department controls the merchandise from the time it is purchased until it is sold to the customers. This department determines what is purchased for sale, how much money will be spent for the merchandise, sales goals, and how to sell the merchandise. You, the VM

1-1 Filene's, Boston MA

designer, must be aware of the merchandise department's selling directives so you can design displays that complement and reinforce sales strategies.

The store's selling staff, the focal point of the merchandising department, create all the sales. Sales people meet the customers, work intimately with the merchandise, and are knowledgeable about their department's directives. In short, the sales staff is a rich source of information for the VM designer. It follows that good communications between the staff and the designer are essential. For example, you can learn from the staff what items are big sellers and what items are slow movers. Knowing this, you can avoid emphasizing sales losers and better spend your time highlighting sales leaders. Remember, fast moving merchandise is your store's sales strength. Additionally, good communications let you assist the sales force with their objectives by training them in good merchandise presentation and display maintenance.

The operating department is not directly involved in the selling of merchandise. Generally, its function is to maintain the company's physical plant and to transport merchandise. Specifically, the operating unit performs such services as: customer home deliveries; building maintenance; in-store housekeeping; merchandise warehousing; transporting merchandise between stores and warehouses; building construction and remodelling; shipping and receiving to and from suppliers; and merchandise marking or price tagging.

For the VM designer, the operating department receives newly purchased display props from manufacturers and stores and transports the props as needed. The department also processes the necessary paperwork asssociated with the receipt, storage and movement of display props. Additionally, the department prepares cost estimates for the VM designer and final cost figures for remodelling projects, as well as providing the maintenance and construction workers necessary to complete such projects.

The fashion merchandising department develops the fashion directions for the store. This department advises the merchandising department about the types and styles of merchandise that should be purchased. It is the fashion group that establishes fashion trends. The VM designer must be familiar with the fashion trends, as they help determine the style of merchandise that is featured on mannequins, presented in display windows, and highlighted in sales departments. Also, knowledge of the trends helps the designer select, buy, and build props to create store environments that support the fashions.

To reinforce fashion trends with the store's customers, the fashion merchandising department schedules in-store fashion shows and events. The responsibility for producing these shows and events falls to the VM designer who must be prepared to provide floor space for the show, chairs, background props, special lighting, sound equipment, runways, signs, and any special effects that may be needed.

The advertising department informs the community about your store and the merchandise it has for sale by preparing and running ads in newspapers and magazines, on radio, TV, and billboards, and by designing catalogs, customer mailers, and other collateral materials. In some instances, the advertising department directs the store's formal public relations program.

The advertising department is staffed with an advertising manager, writers, graphic artists, production manager, media buyers and, in multiple-store operations, a suburban advertising coordinator. The advertising department takes its lead from the merchandising department, which provides information about the products that are to be promoted.

It is absolutely essential that the display staff is at all times aware of the advertising department's activities. The VM designer must highlight advertised products with in-store signs and highly visible displays. It is a waste of money to advertise a product in an effort to generate business, then have customers come into the store and not be able to find the advertised merchandise.

Advertising schedules are planned well in advance of the time that the merchandise is promoted. This lead time gives the display department plenty of opportunity to print signs and create supportive props for featured merchandise. In most stores, monthly schedules that provide a breakdown showing what merchandise will be advertised on a day-to-day basis are provided to the VM designer. You must check those schedules daily to be sure the advertised merchandise is visible and well presented.

At Christmas and other times when there are special sales campaigns or store-wide events, the advertising department designs special art symbols that identify the occasions. (Figure 1-1) For example, the Christmas symbol might be the design of a stylized Christmas tree. This tree can be used throughout the store, appearing in advertisements, on gift boxes and wrapping paper, and used on customer mailers. To broaden customer identification with the symbol and thus the event, the VM designer must use the symbol in its original colors on signs and in-store displays. One variation might be to reproduce the tree as a three-dimensional soft sculpture for window display.

This type of coordination between the advertising department and the visual merchandiser provides strong sales impact. For that matter, whenever the advertising department develops special sales symbols, they should be picked up by the VM designer and repeated in merchandise presentations. The designs and their colors should appear in sales departments, on signs and in other prominent store locations.

In addition to its other services, the advertising department may provide demographic surveys. Generally, these surveys tell you who your customers are, how old they are, where they live, their lifestyles, and ap-

1-2 Marshall Field's, Chicago IL

1-3 Jordan Marsh, Boston MA

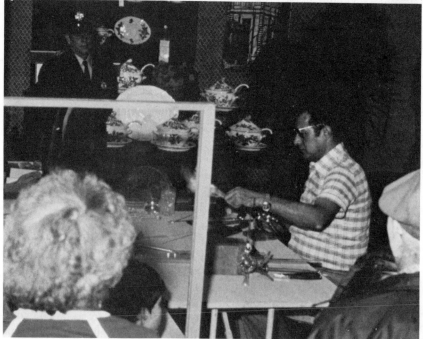

proximately how much money they earn. This information helps the designer decide what fashion statements to make with displays, the price of the merchandise displayed, and the age groups for which the displays should be designed.

The special events department, as the name indicates, arranges all special store functions. These vary from store-wide promotions such as anniversary sales to individual celebrity appearances by apparel designers, authors, artists, sports stars and musicians. (Figure 1-2) A typical appearance is that by an apparel designer who visits the store to talk to customers about designs, helps customers selected merchandise, or hosts a fashion show of the designer's clothes. These events sell great quantities of merchandise, and the store's staff must be prepared to take advantage of the opportunities.

The VM designer must see to it that the merchandise is well presented and grouped close to or surrounding the show site. All merchandise must be identified by signs, special displays, and window displays. Special merchandise fixtures may be needed. The guest celebrity might ask for special lighting, sound equipment, music, and graphics, all of which the VM designer will be expected to provide. Individual cash registers and package wrapping stations are often set up to handle the added sales volume. Crowd control is essential for a successful event. Customer traffic patterns should be planned in advance and controlled by roped-off aisles and show areas. For the most part, members of the special events department will keep the VM designer informed about all the requirements for any given event.

To give you some idea of an event's sales potential, a guest glass blower demonstrating his craft can produce $30,000 in additional sales on the day he appears for the department featuring his wares. (Figure 1-3) And the appearance usually only lasts for three or four hours during the day. With this kind of sales potential, it is vital that you pick the best possible location in the store for the event. A poor location can kill customer enthusiasm. Use plenty of signs announcing the event and directing customers to it. There is no substitute for thorough planning for a special event. Keep in mind that these events produce increased customer traffic and merchandise sales; be prepared for both. A by-product of a special event is the interest in the increased sales shown by members of adjacent departments. This affords the VM designer an opportunity to upgrade displays in these departments to help them maximize sales.

The accounting department is the keeper of the company books. It provides operating capital for the VM department. It handles all your financial transactions and prepares printed records of expenditures to help you control costs and stay within budgetary limits. Best of all, the accounting department writes the payroll checks.

The personnel department is responsible for company-employee relations. It hires the staff, accounts for payroll budgets, maintains personnel

15

files, counsels employees, conducts labor negotiations, holds exit interviews, establishes store-employee policies, records employee payroll time, schedules vacations, and trains employees. The personnel department provides training aids for meetings and assists in teaching employees seasonal presentation strategies.

The visual merchandising department presents all the merchandise to the customers. This is done with window displays, in-department displays, the arrangement of merchandise on selling fixtures, production of special and fashion events, store appearances, and store planning and remodeling.

Display planning begins before the merchandise arrives in the store. The VM designer checks stock and spread sheets to see what merchandise has been purchased and when it is expected to be displayed for sale. The VM designer may gather information about the merchandise, such as color and fabric stories, by previewing the merchandise at market when it is purchased. This data is reviewed well in advance of the merchandise going on display to provide sufficient time for the VM designer to get special fixtures, mannequins and props, prepare signs, allocate floor space, and make any necessary architectural changes.

Planning can be the difference between a great display and a run-of-the-mill display. Advance planning gives the designer a better opportunity to target displays to as many customers as possible: the customers who buy to replace items; the customers who buy items because they need them; the customers who buy out of sheer desire for the items; and the customers who buy items on impulse. Desire and impulse are the least understood sales factors, but they are thought to have unlimited sales potential.

To keep an in-department display as sales effective as possible, it must be maintained. This job falls to the sales staff, as the VM designer has other things to do and cannot spend all his time at a single location. It is up to the VM designer to inform the sales staff about the display and the importance of its maintenance. This is done by holding sales staff meetings, informal conversations, video demonstrations, and by sending memos. Communications with the staff lets the VM designer explain why the merchandise is displayed in a particular manner. For example, a meeting might be held to explain why all woolen apparel is grouped together, its various categories, styles, and colors, and why certain accessories are shown with the woolens. In effect, the staff gains an understanding of the display function. Without this information, they may ignore an essential sales tool.

Help may come to the VM designer from cosmetic, apparel, and home furnishings manufacturers when these companies embark on national sales campaigns. They supply posters, display props, fixtures, and signs that tie-in with their extensive advertising programs. The VM designer decides the quantities of promotional materials and types of displays that are needed to supplement such efforts. Well-identified displays that reflect national campaigns can produce record-breaking sales.

The VM designer who works for a store located in a large shopping plaza will probably be asked to work with the plaza merchants' association. This group sets plaza store standards and prepares promotions to create customer traffic. Every association has an events director who plans four or five annual events that range from antique auto shows to art fairs, flower shows to orchestra concerts. The largest of these is usually held at Christmas. The VM designer helps the director plan some of the events and ofen may be called on to assist in securing resources to pay for the event decorations. Within the store, it is a good idea for the VM designers to create presentations that inform the customers about the upcoming plaza event. These presentations can be as simple as a sign or as complex as displaying an event feature such as an antique automobile along with tie-in merchandise. Some events may require one or two window displays.

The display director may be called upon to provide design ideas for a store float that will be used in an Easter or Christmas parade. This is a very specialized business, and it is probably best to call in a firm that builds floats to execute the VM designer's ideas.

A local restauranteur may contact the store about holding a fashion show in his restaurant that features the store's merchandise. If the show is approved, it will be produced by the VM designer, who must plan for models, the merchandise to be modelled, transportation for the models, on-site fitting rooms with makeup mirrors, model traffic patterns within the restaurant, and signs promoting the store. The store's fashion department will help the designer by planning the show fashion theme and picking the models, as well as the clothes and accessories they will wear.

Occasionally, the VM designer will be asked to give talks about his work to clubs and school groups. If the talk is to a retail association, it should be very professional. Slide presentations are most helpful. The advertising or visual departments can help by providing visual aids.

In multiple-store companies, the visual merchandising department is usually headed by a VM vice president who reports to the company president. The VM vice president has a staff that includes store planners, VM managers, designers, and secretarial staff. The VM managers are the people who manage the display departments in individual stores. They functionally report to the store managers, but receive policy and artistic directions from the VM vice president and his staff. Since the VM department is responsible to the merchandising group, a member of the VM vice president's staff is normally assigned to the merchandising department to ensure that merchandise presentation standards are maintained.

In some companies, the VM staff is itinerate. That is, the company has a VM vice president, whose central manager and staff travel from store to store to handle all display functions.

A word about semantics here is appropriate to avoid later confusion. The term "visual merchandising" refers to all the activities associated with

1-4 Bachman's, Minneapolis MN

1-5 Bachman's, Minneapolis MN

merchandise presentation such as setting-up merchandise displays, presentation policies, artistic directions, budgetary management, and employee supervision. Years ago, the word "display" was used to describe the designer's function. However, as the display designer's responsibilities increased, the word "display" became an inadequate description of the job. A broader term was needed, so "visual merchandising" came into vogue.

Today "display" has a narrow meaning that refers to the actual work involved in presenting merchandise, such as changing a mannequin or arranging materials in a window. However, it should be noted that some stores still use the word "display" when describing their VM departments.

Visual merchandising can be the factor that determines whether a store or its competitor sells merchandise to a customer. This is because suppliers, with few exceptions, make all their merchandise available to all stores. Therefore, it is difficult to buy merchandise that is exclusive to any one store. The difference between one store and another is the manner in which the store presents its merchandise to customers.

As more and more merchandise is offered to customers on a self-selection basis, it is important that the merchandise be presented in such a way as to make it easy for the customer to make selections. (Figure 1-4) That is, the order of merchandise should be arranged to emphasize categories that establish price, highlight fashion and color trends, reflect age groups and lifestyles, or any desirable grouping that creates customer awareness. Proper presentation glamourizes the merchandise, creates hard or soft-sell environments, and establishes store traffic patterns. (Figure 1-5)

Window displays are a good medium to communicate a high fashion or trendy message to the customers. Windows are also excellent for signalling store special events and sales to the public. Well positioned mannequins tell customers about the fashions to be found in the department, how to put the fashion "looks" together, and what accessories to select for use with them. Mannequins help customers make up their minds about various fashions. Merchandise on fixtures, grouped together, informs customers about dress combinations, colors, and fabrics. These displays, in addition to featuring merchandise and informing customers, also help project the store's image.

The store image is a reflection of the type of merchandise the store has for sale. For example, the image tells customers whether it is an exclusive men's shop, a discount store, or a jeans shop. (Figure 1-6) The image must be keyed closely to the community in which the store is located. For example, it might be appropriate to have an exclusive shop in some neighborhoods, but not in others. It is important to project sub-categories of merchandise, but the overall store image is established by impacting merchandise strengths and strong sellers.

With fewer sales people to explain the store merchandise attitudes, it is crucial that customers assimilate this information from displays. It requires

1-6 John A. Brown, Oklahoma City OK

1-7 Lytton's, Chicago IL

a great deal of time and expertise to provide this data through displays, so as a result, the VM designer spends most of his time working on the store interior. It is no wonder efforts are being made to make window displays easier and less costly to install. People spend less time shopping, so it behooves the VM designer to create displays that immediately project the store image, merchandise categories, and price points. (A "price point" is the retail price of the product.)

Some customers are very knowledgeable about fashions, and their advanced requirements may necessitate special merchandise presentations. In general, merchandise presentations should cater to the tastes and pocketbooks of the majority of the customers. (Figure 1-7)

Customers trust store images and believe that whatever merchandise is stocked, advertised, and displayed is in fashion. On the other hand, customers lose faith in a store if they find their purchases, made on the basis of displays, are not fashionable. Fashion trend information is passed along to the VM designer from the fashion merchandising department. It takes cooperation between all management groups to project and protect a store's image.

To impact fashion images upon customers, do not clutter merchandise presentations with superfluous display props. For example, to present better sportswear, arrange a group of four or five well-dressed mannequins at the front of the sportswear department. Locate a hanging rack holding the same fashions by the side of the mannequins and identify the display with a clear, highly-visible sign. This method of highlighting merchandise begins to tell the sportswear story.

It is just as easy for customers to see and think about the merchandise on five mannequins in a group as it is to think about the merchandise on one. All the items on the mannequins should be the products from one manufacturer. Do not mix colors. Use yellow, if yellow is the fashion color, and repeat the color family on all mannequins. Do not add reds, greens, or whites. To avoid monotony, use solid colors on some mannequins and muted prints on others, and vary the fashion tops and bottoms — that is, skirts, blouses and jackets. Dress all mannequins in fashions having the same fabrics, textures, and sleeve length (profile). The fashions should emphasize the activity for which they were designed, whether for active sports or late afternoon wear. Also, the merchandise on the mannequins should have the same price points.

Stock all racks around the display using the same guidelines that were used to dress the mannequins. Each rack should have only the fashions from one manufacturer, and in the same colors, fabrication, and profile. (Figure 1-8) Clutter is created if the fashions on the same rack have varying sleeve lengths. Show all blouses together, skirts together and jackets together on separate racks and the fashion story becomes clear. Customers should not have to search through all the apparel to find items of their choice. Price points should be identical on individual fixtures. Even beyond a particular display, these same stocking guidelines should be maintained throughout a department for all merchandise. Supportive fixtures, wall colors, and graphics can add emphasis to a fashion message.

Here is an additional idea about impacting merchandise. Red T-shirts, for example, look better when displayed together on face-outs rather than on round racks where the customers see only the shirt sleeves. As with all merchandise, keep the shirt colors separate on different racks; do not make a display less effective by showing shirts in all colors on the same racks. The use of the guidelines will leave no doubt in the minds of the customers as to what the VM designer is emphasizing.

Merchandise sales are made by the sales staff and it is rather easy to document individuals' productivity. Sales records are maintained on an hourly, daily, weekly, monthly, and yearly basis. The staff selling costs can be readily computed. On the other hand, it is extremely difficult if not impossible to pinpoint sales generated by merchandise presentations. However, it is known that the way in which merchandise is presented, highlighted, and impacted can increase or decrease the salability of the goods. Merchandise presentation establishes customer awareness. Non-selling and slow moving categories will begin to sell when properly displayed to the customers.

Merchandise displays are informative, particularly when introducing new products. Fashions change quickly and customers rely on store presentations to keep them abreast of the latest styles. Fashion displays should be changed frequently to remind customers of the many fashion statements the store makes. The timing for changing other product displays is not as critical as it is for fashions. Styles shown on mannequins can be changed every few days or weekly, but fashions shown on costumers and highlight fixtures should be reviewed and changed daily or whenever new merchandise arrives.

Arrange merchandise on highlight fixtures in order of manufacturer, color, texture, profile and price. Resist the temptation to arrange merchandise by garment size. Initially, customers come into the store looking for an apparel attitude, color and price. When they find this merchandise, they will then select the sizes they need. Size arranging promotes the weakest merchandise characteristic to the customers and generates the cluttered look. The VM designer must review the store's daily newspaper advertisements to be sure the advertised merchandise, along with appropriate signs, is shown in a conspicuous location.

Studies show that in-store displays make customers more aware of fashion trends than any other medium. Advertising is limited to the number of persons who see and read it. Also, advertising illustrates the merchandise in a two-dimensional drawing or photo. The impact of fashion shows is limited by their duration and the number of customers who are

1-8 Saks, Manhattan NY

able to attend. In-store displays have the advantage of showing the merchandise as three-dimensional products that customers can view from all angles, see the colors, and touch the fabrics. This is not to say that advertising and fashion shows should be eliminated. They are very important sales tools and quite necessary for complete sales programs.

There are many departments in a large store and these departments contain many categories of merchandise. In this complex structure, it is not unusual for some items to lose their visibility. Occasionally, customers cannot find sales items if they have not been impacted by the VM designer.

To design displays that maximize product awareness, always work with product strengths. Every product has features such as color, type of construction, utility, and price that can make the product a strong seller. It is generally true that presentation of the strongest product categories and biggest income producers generate the strongest sales. A product that is not potentially a strong seller should receive less promotion effort. The time spent trying to promote a weak product only lessens the time available to promote the winners. It is more profitable to create customer interest in products that have a sales potential of $10,000 than it is to create interest in a product that has a $2,000 sales potential. Also, a product that is a loser requires more effort than a simple display to sell it.

Members of the merchandising department help the VM designer select the products that will be displayed. Weekly meetings with the merchandising group keep the VM designer informed about merchandising policies, sales goals, upcoming advertising and product promotions. The merchandising group determines sales directions which the designer translates into presentation techniques. Some sales goals are planned six months to a year in advance, while others are planned on a week-to-week basis.

Merchandise information can be gathered from the sales staff; they know which products are potentially the best sellers, which have just arrived in the store, customer attitudes, the effectiveness of in-department presentations, day-to-day display needs, which fixtures are obsolete and which need repairs. The sales staff also knows the products that need special fixtures and where best to locate those fixtures in the department.

The VM manager begins the day by touring the store to see that all mannequins are dressed in the latest fashions and all displays are neat and orderly. Further checks are made to be sure all the day's advertised merchandise is highlighted and identified by proper signs, that all outdated signs are removed, and that all fixtures are in good repair. It is very important that the store has all the signs that are needed. If any are missing or contain errors, the VM manager's staff will make replacements. After the tour, the VM manager meets briefly with the store manager to find out if any last minute displays have been scheduled and to discuss the day's sales strategies.

Next comes the display staff meeting where the VM manager can review sales goals and merchandising directions and plan work assignments for the day. The fashion and special events schedule indicates any events to be staged and any special fashions to be presented. The window schedule indicates the window displays to be changed and the category of merchandise to be shown in the new displays. The store interior schedule indicates the mannequins to be changed and any special store displays to be set up.

The balance of the day is spent helping department heads allocate space for new merchandise, arranging fixtures and supportive display items, directing the VM staff in creating displays, locating props, producing artwork for displays, reviewing budgets, attending to personnel problems, meeting with prop and fixture suppliers, and ordering the supplies necessary to operate the VM department. □

2

Principles of Design

Display is one commercial art form that allows the designer to work with all art forms to achieve his or her design. The merchandise and supportive materials used to create a display include an assemblage of the following elements:

A. Graphics. Panels made of fabric, plexi, and wood, foam core composition board, and fabric are used as backdrop for the merchandise. (Figure 2-1) These panels create a mood for the merchandise, as well as segregating the display from surrounding materials and adjacent merchandise. Generally, they are hung from a ceiling in a vertical manner; however, they might be supported on a floor or fastened to a sculpted composition. The panels could be graphic designs, lettering, photos, fashion illustrations, fabric design, collage, bas-relief, posters, wallpaper, solid color or anything that relates to the mood of the merchandise. These panels must relate to the color, texture, use, price, or any outstanding feature of the merchandise.

B. Fine Arts. The backdrop panels can be in the form of a painting or a photograph from the store gallery. (Figures 2-2 and 2-3) In small scale, they can be combined with the merchandise in the display as a tool for assisting the composition and arrangement of merchandise.

C. Color. This is the most important art element used. It will be the cohesive factor in your composition, allowing combinations of diverse materials such as velvet and vinyl, wood and wool, tweed and toile. Color can evoke a mood, relate to a period, tie in with the function of the mer-

2-1 Marshall Field's, Calumet City IL

chandise, and help you balance your composition.

D. Texture. The surface of all objects suggests texture, which can range from smooth to rough. The total display can suggest an overall texture. (Figure 2-4) Ninety percent of the texture used in a composition should be similar. Diverse textures can be added, but in small amounts so as not to disturb the dominant textural theme. Heavily textured wool products can be combined with nubby primitive antique furniture, establishing the dominant theme. All major dominant textures must be similar. Smooth glass, leather, and pottery can be added to this group of rough textures for design relief in small amounts as an accent. If equal amounts of opposite textures are used, you will confuse the texture signal and weaken your composition.

E. Photography. Large photo blowups used as a display backdrop will be mood-creating for the merchandise. Combined with the merchandise as an accessory, they can tell a story about the goods and be used as an object to balance your composition. The subject, period, and color of the photo blowup should relate to the dominant characteristics of the merchandise.

F. Lettering. Many letters are beautifully designed, and as a graphic art form they can make a display backdrop. (Figure 2-5) Signs are used to describe and price merchandise. Whether used in a display as an art object or as a sign to price merchandise, the type style and color should relate to your compositional theme.

G. Lighting. With light we see the display and determine its color. If the in-store display is lighted with general store lighting, most of the dramatic effect is lost. Additional lighting must be used to impact the look. Very special lighting is required in a window to help create the mood, emphasize color balance, and to make it bright enough to be seen. Good window lighting will help you highlight the feature qualities of your design and merchandise.

H. Balance. The proper positioning of the merchandise, combined with signs and display materials in the form of artwork, will establish good balance and a pleasant visual effect. (Figure 2-6) Color, texture, and lighting are tools to help you properly balance your display. Proper balance, establishing focal points, can highlight the merchandise in your display.

I. Drawing. Whether drawing a floor plan or elevation or creating an illustration for your display, you will use drawing techniques and styles. The need for simple sketches to illustrate your design concept, or a sophisticated fashion illustration as part of the display, will make you want to develop your drawing skills. Technical floor plans and elevations are needed to guide tradespeople in the installation of displays, shops, fixture placement, rug laying, lighting, painting, remodelling, and new construction. One must be able to draw simple floor plans and interpret these drawings. (Figure 2-7)

J. Painting. Drawing and painting scenery enables you to make your own display props. All media are available to you, as well as periods, styles, and subject matter. Painting a period landscape and using it as a backdrop, along with a similar painting, helps reinforce the style of the merchandise. The color, texture, balance, subject matter, and style of the paintings must relate to the dominant theme of your merchandise.

K. Art History. Since all of the elements in a display — merchandise, artwork, color, design, and balance — all relate to a historical period, one must have a basic knowledge of art history. The colors and balance of toile, for example, reflect the designer's solution to a design problem in the 1700's. You must pick up on these design symbols, repeating them in the display, to emphasize the product. Anytime you repeat texture, color, line, balance, or any design element, you give it strength and impact. When designing period displays, repeat the obvious symbols of that period. (Figure 2-8)

Merchandise is three dimensional, and except for a window display, the design will be viewed from all angles. One must begin to think like a sculptor and consider all angles of the display — front, back, and sides — for good design.

All the merchandise has been inspired, created, and shaped by a designer who has used the above design principles. You must identify the best design features in the merchandise, such as shape, color or pattern and repeat them in the display. They will produce harmony between the merchandise and the display materials, and together they will create the strong impact you desire.

FORM

Three dimensional form, roundness or squareness, is emphasized by light, shade, color, and texture. (Figure 2-9) An assemblage of merchandise with all these dimensional characteristics creates the display. The display itself is round or square, having been made of a harmonious collection of parts. This dimensional display can be condensed, with all parts close together creating a shallow depth. Items spaced at a greater distance in a display will create greater depth. It is often effective to have all items on one line to create a flat plane or shallow depth. This composition should consist of smooth textures to emphasize this flat quality, but it is not all-important. If one is displaying heavily textured sweaters, for example, in a shallow display space, concentrate on diminishing the sweaters' roundness so they relate to the flat plane.

Form can establish a mood — the form of perfume containers and packages suggests a delicate mood, the form of men's sweaters suggests a rugged mood. Flat forms might suggest the mood of a quiet summer day. An object can be identified by its form, for example, the shape of a plate suggests china. When you are composing a china display, you could use many round items similar in color and texture to emphasize the roundness of the plates. If you are displaying seventy pieces of china, you would consider the overall form of bulk china. Make and select supportive display materials to emphasize its bulk.

A large product is the display's focal point; smaller items in contrasting size are the supportive elements. All elements, if similar in color and texture, will help support your composition. You will intensify the look of the display by repeating the basic shape, color, and texture of the focal point and the supportive elements.

To achieve perspective in a display, place the merchandise along traditional perspective lines. Depth depends on your emphasis. A small floor plan sketch of the display indicating perspective lines will help you in organizing this.

TEXTURE

The surface of an object produces a tactile and visual sensation. The texture of an object is in character with its form and use. Sensitivity to texture is important in determining the material's use. When combining textures, choose a definite relationship, one to another. The grain of wood, the fibrous look of wool, the smoothness of glass and metal reveal a quality of the product and relate to its use. (Figures 2-10 and 2-11)

Texture is synonymous with period. An eighteenth century highboy has a definite texture, in contrast to the sleek glass and steel of contemporary furniture. Sleek steely textures pervade all art forms of the modern period. When designing a period display, one must use all the textures that relate to and are identified by that period. If doing an adaptation or up-dated period display, non-period textures can be combined, but not in significant amounts that will disturb the identity of the period. One texture look should dominate the display about seventy to eighty percent. This ratio will develop order in your display.

Mood is communicated by texture: a silk fabric suggests refinement; a woolen tweed suggests casualness.

A dress may be made of textured wool, but have sleek metal buttons and a soft synthetic collar. This combination presents a mixture of textures. The texture of the dress fabric dominates by about ninety percent, the buttons and collar are accent textures supporting five percent or less of the dress. In your display design, do not strongly repeat the least significant textures. Wool is the dominant texture of the dress and should be repeated in the display in the same ratio as it is used in the product. The accent textures (the steel of the buttons and synthetic collar) should appear not more than five percent, if at all.

LINE

Form is defined by line. A sculptor, after shaping the form of a man, will define hair and the facial characteristics by line drawing into the clay with his tool. Some line is non-existent, imaginary. The position of a shoe and a purse in a display makes the eye follow one object to another, creating a compositional line. These imaginary lines are important because they keep the eye involved in the display. Compositional lines developed by proper merchandise placement will keep the eye moving from product to product

2-2 Carson Pirie Scott, Chicago IL

2-3 Carson Pirie Scott, Chicago IL

34

2-5 Marshall Field's, Calumet City IL

2-6 Hart Schaffner & Marx, Chicago IL

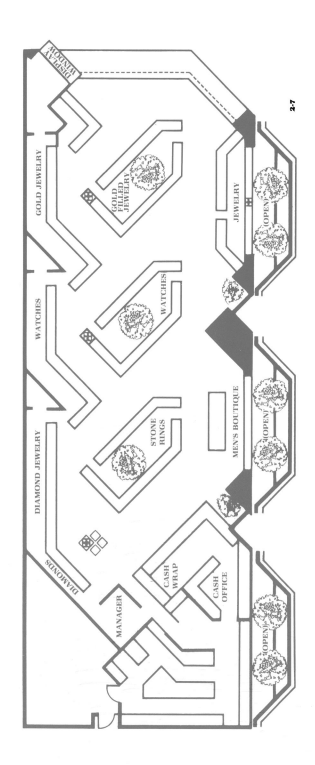

DISPLAY WINDOW

GOLD JEWELRY

GOLD FILLED JEWELRY

WATCHES

WATCHES

DIAMOND JEWELRY

STONE RINGS

DIAMONDS

MANAGER

CASH WRAP

CASH OFFICE

MEN'S BOUTIQUE

JEWELRY

(OPEN)

(OPEN)

(OPEN)

2-7

2-8 W. J. Sloane, San Francisco CA

2-9 Lipton's, Toronto, Ontario

2-10 Marshall Field's, Calumet City IL

2-11 Marshall Field's, Calumet City IL

2-12 Madigan's, River Forest IL

2-13 Marshall Field's, Calumet City IL

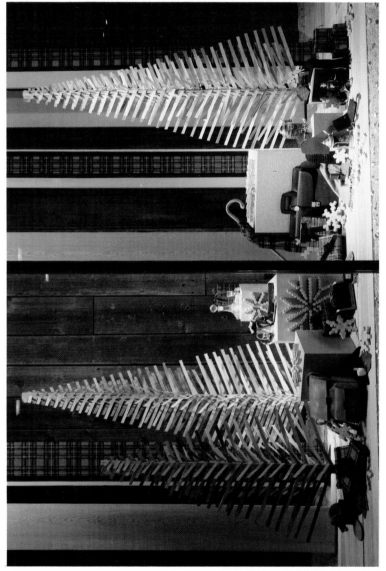

2-14 Marshall Field's, Calumet City IL

2-15 Gimbels, New York NY

2-16 Bergdorf Goodman, New York NY

2-17 Bullock's, San Mateo CA

2-18 Magasin du Nord, Arhus, Denmark

2-19 Grace Bros., Broadway NSW Australia

2-20 Marshall Field's, Calumet City IL.

2-21 Madigan's, River Forest IL

2-22 Marshall Field's, Calumet City IL

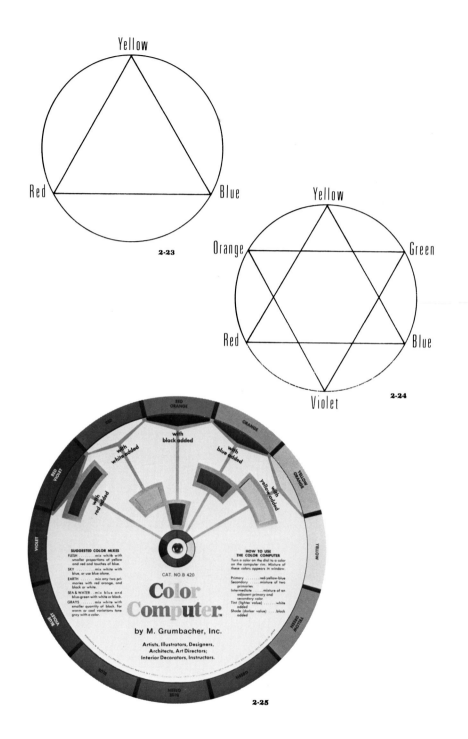

2-23

2-24

2-25

and prevent it from leaving the display.

Line will define space. Color and textural lines created by merchandise placement on the floor of a display window will carry your eye to the back, thus establishing perspective. The eye moves progressively from one color or textural repeat on to the back of your display. The imaginary line from one object to another will carry your eye through space. (Figure 2-12) The linear pattern of the product and the display materials create mood. They should relate closely. The delicate lines of a dress fabric combined with a delicate drawing can evoke sensitivity. Specific, sharp lines suggest action, softer lines suggest tranquility. These lines suggest a quality and identity about the product. The dominant linear quality should be repeated clearly. Diverse linear patterns in your display in equal amounts suggesting action and tranquility will create a confusing image.

An Art Deco dress should be combined with an Art Deco product with similar linear quality. These products must be synonomous with the period and mood of the dress. There are many Art Deco products that will complement the dress such as compacts, shoes, purses, scarves, cosmetics, drawings, paintings, and home furnishings.

The line that defines a floral country chintz is different than the line that defines a contemporary flower. The thickness of the line, how it repeats, its shape, how it outlines the object, etc., all suggest period style, quality, and identify the object. Lines repeating in a vertical manner can create a static balance, lines repeating at an angle can create an action image, lines curvaceous and soft can create a relaxed image. Line can be used to create texture: repeated hatch lines create roughness; repeated curved lines create softness. Repeated lines can identify a pattern and a mood. Line appears in all objects, and is a great tool to control and develop your composition. There must be order in the way you use line. You must generate a great interrelationship in the linear quality of display materials and products that you choose and develop. There is the linear quality of the product and accessories, as well as that established by the whole display composition. Line is the basis of all design.

Contour line illustrates that what we are seeing is a tree, for example. Repeated textural line defines the bark. Lacy lines illustrate and identify the branches. Vertical lines illustrate its height. Circular lines illustrate its thickness. When the tree is surrounded by lines that illustrate other trees, the image and profile is blurred. You see a forest rather than a single tree. Some degree of contrast helps us see the uniqueness of the object, but great amounts of contrast overpower the object.

BALANCE

One would think that it takes two items to balance a composition, but compositional balance can be achieved by balancing one product with blank space. (Figure 2-13) In a composition, all space is viewed. Negative space (the blank, empty space between objects) adds to the whole of the display. If two products are too close together while others are equally spaced, you will break the artistic rythmn. To achieve harmony with negative space, one must think of negative space as pattern. Design the negative space so the pattern is harmonious with the product placement.

Sometimes it is important to have one product in the window. That product can be positioned on the side to eliminate static balance. Balance the blank space with the product. The product is positive; blank space is negative. One must think of the total space and balance these two elements properly.

Balance should follow the natural axis of the display window. Some display windows have a definite vertical or horizontal design. The balance in a vertical window should be vertical and in a horizontal window use horizontal balance.

One large product positioned to the side can be counter-balanced by several small items. A static balance is created by placing two items of equal size beside each other on the same sight line. (Figure 2-14) Less static results if you move one of the items back a few inches. Three dimensional design allows great possibility and variation with balance. Mood is established by balance. Static balance can illustrate strength and formality. Informal balance can create action. Off-balance can illustrate tension.

Balance can be used to create an overall pattern. A circular arrangement on a flat surface will create an active mood. Items arranged in a circle on the floor plane will illustrate action and depth. Items can be arranged three dimensionally to illustrate solid geometric patterns such as the cube, pyramid, and sphere. A two-dimensional arrangement on a flat surface creates a circle, a square, or a triangle. In combination they create complete geometric forms. An old display design balance method has been to repeat all similar objects in groups of three. The three objects must be similar in size, theme and shape.

SPACE

The space you work with in a display window or an in-store display location is the volume visual plane and must be organized. A simple sketch, elevation drawing, and floor plan must be prepared to help determine the proper measurements of the space. The merchandise and accessories must fit the space. Sometimes a product will look different in size on the selling floor. The product can be too large or too small, causing a problem when trying to arrange it in the display space. The selling space is often quite large, distorting one's concept about the product's size. Display areas are much smaller than selling areas and to avoid problems measure everything, including height, depth, and width. Remember, you are dealing with volume design in all three dimensions. The drawings will help develop a composition for the space.

In organizing the design of the display space, you must apply the use of color, line, balance, texture, and all the design principles. In organizing these elements, you are composing the design. A compositional sketch will be your tool in planning all that happens in the display space. Begin the sketch by arranging the merchandise in combination with the supportive merchandise such as paintings, artwork, and display materials. A detailed elevation drawing will organize and compose all that happens on the visual plane from floor to ceiling. Drawing a floor plan will let you plan and compose the third dimension. All that happens from side to side and from front to back.

If the products are small in relation to the scale of the display space, then the display space must be reduced. The space can be shortened in height and depth, as well as width. The fast way of reducing space is to fly or hang decorative foam core panels — plain, colored, patterned or illustrated.

The display space is your canvas. The volume design is expressed by an interplay of planes, some of which are more prominent because of their size, position, shape, and color, while others look as if they recede. The visual height is expressed by a vertical plane. The arrangement on the floor expresses the horizontal plane. The floor should not be overlooked — its size is significant and should receive design consideration. Flooring material, cork, mats, and rugs must relate to the whole design in their color, texture, scale, theme, line, volume, and quality. Plan the position of the merchandise and related materials on the horizontal plane of the the floor.

The use of transparent and opaque materials increases our sensitivity to what happens between two solids. Great textural relationships are created in space by their juxtaposition. Depth and height are expressed by their relationship. The purpose of design unity is to focus interest on the display so that it fills the whole field of attention. The display must stand out separately from other objects within the field of vision.

The relationship between the horizontal and vertical planes can create tension, illustrating an active mood, or harmony, illustrating a subdued mood.

When one faces a blank sheet of drawing paper, it is hard to be inspired. Design ideas are difficult to develop. A good guideline is to let the merchandise totally inspire design ideas about the display. The term "merchandise design theme" spells out this process. If you think about the product — its use, design, quality, style, and color — you will come up with enough ideas to help develop the display design, strengthening merchandise presentation.

Here is an example of the product inspiring a presentation idea. A sexy red purse, placed on a counter makes a statement; a red compact placed next to the purse, makes the statement stronger. Add a red cigarette holder and a red packaged lipstick and it is beginning to make an impact. Add a red scarf and a pair of red shoes and it has created a strong impact. This is achieved by repeating the obvious design element of the red purse, its color. This type of presentation — the collection of similar merchandise such as a scarf, shoe and so forth — is called a "lifestyle presentation." If you are presenting a purse classification, the same principle applies. The red purse is significant; two red purses make a stronger statement; twenty red purses together create a strong impact. Color repeat has impacted the purse classification.

In the store, there are some product classifications that should be mass merchandised and others that are more exclusive. Exclusive merchandise that sells for high price points should not be presented in large quantities. This can turn the customer off. You must evaluate your merchandise policies and modify impacting by quantity. For exclusivity, instead of showing fifteen pairs of the same gold earrings, show all styles of gold earrings together to create impact. The gold earring collection as a whole is the classification.

COLOR

Designers use a different color order than expressed by physicists. Our colors includes five color families — red, blue, yellow, green, and the neutrals. Each family has two varieties, warm and cool.

A. **Red.** Its warm variety is yellow (orange), its cool variety is blue (purple). The red family is warm.

Yellow	Blue
Warm	Cool

B. **Blue.** Its warm variety is red (royal blue), its cool variety is green (turquoise). The blue family is cool.

Red	Green
Warm	Cool

C. **Yellow.** Its warm variety is red (orange), its cool variety is green (avocado). The yellow family is warm.

Red	Green
Warm	Cool

D. **Green.** Its warm variety is yellow (spring green), its cool variety is blue (aqua). The green family is cool.

Yellow	Blue
Warm	Cool

E. **Neutrals.** Their warm varieties are yellow and red; their cool varieties are green and blue. Neutral color families can be warm or cool.

The Red Family

Red is a warm color family — it gets hotter as it becomes orange, a bit cooler as it becomes blue. Blue-red and yellow-red are not always compatible. They are opposites, even though they are within the red family. If you mix blue-red and yellow-red paint together, it will produce gray-red. The blue and yellow in the red cancel each other because they are opposite colors.

Red is a conspicuous color. It signals excitement. Red becomes pastel by adding white and it becomes gray by adding black. This has a subduing effect on the color's impact; for example, pink is a pastel red and is not as conspicuous as pure red. Color will evoke a mood more than any other design elements. The mood of late-day reds are mellow, as opposed to more fragile early morning reds — each red expresses a different mood. Bright reds are synonomous with action.

The red family is effected by texture. Red shaggy wool produces a robust look; the same red on silk a refined look, and on glass a shiny, sophisticated look. This allows the designer to vary the look while using the same color family. Variety within the family can be created by changing its value. Gray-red is less conspicuous. The more blue in the red, the cooler it is, the more yellow, the hotter it is. Pure red is a powerful color to use in an interior in quantity. Look at upholstery fabric and interior paint samples and you will quickly observe that they are grayed or pastel. They are quiet red varieties easy to live with. Red sportswear is grayed in winter and brighter in summer. Vendors package their products in red for impact.

It is good to use red in a display, but unwise to paint a whole department red. Red walls will overpower the merchandise. (Figure 2-15)

Red can move a compositional plane forward, allowing you another dimension in designing a display.

All the oranges of the red-yellow variety are included in the red family. When the color signals more yellow than red, it belongs in the yellow family. Wood colors are a part of the red family as manifested by red-browns or the warm neutrals. Purples of the red-blue variety are included in the red family. As these cooler reds signal more blue than red, they belong to the blue family. (Figure 2-16)

Red is a romantic color, as in a red rose or candlelight. Color will evoke a theme quicker than any other element. One can be mildly excited by Louis XV furniture or Chippendale, but one is totally absorbed by color. The furniture design impact is weaker than the color impact.

The red family is considered a natural family. It is found in nature, and enhances wood tones, food, and skin colors. Red has become a favorite for restaurant interiors and backgrounds that enhance people and foods.

Red and green are opposites. Green, green-blue, or strong green-yellow in their pure form will fight with red. To make them compatible, gray them or make them pastel. Pale green and pink make a lovely combination. Changing the value reduces the redness of red and greenness of green. The hue makes less of an impact.

Disperse red evenly through your composition to create balance and avoid a lopsided effect. A poor mix of gray and pastel reds will upset your color story. A whole light, airy, feminine look can be created by the use of pastel reds (pinks). A masculine look can be created by the use of gray or dark reds. Mixing the two values in equal amounts will confuse the image.

One value should dominate by eighty percent.

Periods are identified by color. Deep red was a symbol of the Victorian period. It related to the heavily scaled walnut furniture and textured fabric. Colors do relate to the use and design of the product. A display of period products should be composed of colors that relate to and are associated with that period. Red is a favorite color for decorative art. When the fine art trends were decorative in a period, red was the artist's favorite palette.

A color can be a favorite for a national group or climate. The red used in interiors and on clothing around the equator is in brighter, more intense forms and used as an accent, mostly the yellow variety. Red-blues were the favorites of European royalty.

"Hue" is the name of a color. For example, red is a color name or hue. "Value" describes the lightness or darkness of a color. Pastel red (pink) is the light value of red. "Intensity" is the brightness or dullness of a color. Pure red illustrates the color's intensity. Pink is a light value of red, but may be of an intensity ranging from bright pink to dull pink.

Contrasting the value of red will emphasize contour, calling attention to the object. If a dark red value is used as a background, the lighter red value used in front will appear obvious. When the value range is small, one object blends with the other. White surrounding a hue will make its intensity and value obvious. One is totally aware of the redness of red when white is its background.

The Blue Family

Blue is a cool color. It is the color of ice, water, and the atmosphere, all chilly in effect. Blue is also a receding color. In its pure form, it looks more recessive and heavier than red. (Figure 2-17)

Blue is not a natural color. It is often called a manmade color. Although it appears in nature (in the sky), it is not an earth color. It does not complement food tones, skin colors, or wood colors. The red-blues are the warmest of the family. If you must use blue with wood or skin, use the red varieties. Blue-green is the chilliest variety of the blue family. Orange would be its direct opposite. If these opposite colors are to be combined, change their value.

Dark colored items look small in contrast; items that are light colored look large. The light colored objects reflect light and have the look of being expanded in size. A pure red chair will look larger than a pure blue chair. Blue is a darker, heavier color. This color use will let you control the mass of an object without changing color value. A pure yellow chair will look larger than the red or blue one. In order of dark to light, the color families are blue, green, red, yellow, and the neutrals, except dark grey and black.

The opposite of pure blue is pure yellow, the opposite of blue-red is green-yellow, and the opposite of blue-green is red-yellow. Blue used as a background with its opposite yellow as the foreground will set up a vibrating optical effect. The foreground will become very conspicuous.

Blue symbolizes sophistication. It is hard to think of a sky not being blue. Navy blue is a blue-red, a warm variety grayed in value. Compatible with skin tones, blue jeans are an example. Baby blue is a pastel blue-red, making it a pleasant combination with warm colors and the baby's skin color. Designers will choose all the wood tones in a dominant blue room to be dark or very pale or painted. This de-emphasizes the rich warm look of wood, an opposite color which contrasts with the color of blue.

Blue is a very affected by texture. A lacquered blue box can look sophisticated; the same blue on a deep pile rug looks heavy and rich; and on a blue scarf will look light and airy. Blue on a metal box looks reflective, and on a soft fabric looks diffused. It absorbs light rays more and will fade easier than other colors. It will take greater light intensity to make blue-red objects obvious.

Blue is a great resort color. Blue-green is a summer color used in swimwear and resort apparel. (Figures 2-18 and 2-19) People in equatorial communities love to use blue in their interiors. The darker values are used more in northern climes. Winter apparel is dark blue and the red variety. Except for black, the dark blues and especially the blue-reds look more serious than other colors.

Blue was a favorite accent color family used in American Georgian eighteenth century rooms. It was used in samll amounts (about fifteen percent) on accessory items. The great Chinese export china was decorated with blue-red. This china filled open cupboards. Blue used in this way was considered in accent color. An accent color is one used in small amounts, often brighter and sometimes an opposite of the dominant color theme. Accent colors are used in amounts of about ten to fifteen percent. They should not overpower or dominate the major color theme. The amount of blue used as an accent color in Georgian rooms was never strong enough to interfere with all the great wood colors, pine floors, Honduras mahogany chair frames and rich wood panelling. Combined with blue, pale yellow was the other Georgian accent color. Pale red-yellow upholstery, fresh and fragile, produced the warmth to flatter the Honduras mahogany reddish-brown wooden chair frames.

Blue has always been a favorite color of designers for decorating china. They always used blue-red in small amounts. The white of the china contributed about eighty percent of the color, making it the dominant color. White was chosen as a dominant because it supported the food colors. The twenty percent blue of the china was never enought to contrast with the food. The most conspicuous and obvious color of a product or an interior is not always the dominant color. All color on an object must be considered. The one that makes the greatest contribution or appears most is the dominant color. The one that contributes the least is the accent color.

Blue is very visible against a white background. It makes a good

55

substitute color for black lettering on signs.

Blue floral prints have always been used as cottage prints. The blue floral is found on a field of white. Blue is the most obvious, but it is really an accent color. White is the dominant color, making the floral pattern look crisp and fresh.

The Neutral Color Family

Beige, white, gray, black, mushroom, and brown make up this color family. The neutrals do not demand or dictate color. Because the color image is weak, the surface quality of an object is dominant. (Figure 2-20) The texture of objects is made more significant with neutrals than with any other color family. There is no color impact to distract you from the object's surface. Color is a most personal choice. Some people are not comfortable with some of the color families. The neutrals are a good background for store departments because they allow merchandise itself to impact. The neutrals evoke less image and tend to disturb customers less.

There are warm and cool neutral varieties. White and black can be warm or cool, depending on its basic color makeup. A white with a green or blue base will be cool; with a base of yellow or red will be warm.

One cannot think about the neutrals without thinking of the textural quality of grass cloth, glass, metal, shaggy carpets, and frosty silk. The mood created by these textural combinations can be equal to the mood established by a color family. Excitement is created by combining rough woods, metals, and smooth glass. Combinations of closely related textures, silk, smooth glass, velvet, and metal can create a tranquil mood. The quality and use of the product can be established by texture. A fur lined cup would be a disaster. Shiny steel cars suggest strength and ease of maintenance.

The neutral colors are great tranquil background colors or overall colors for stores, household interiors, work spaces, and public rooms. They are affected less by the fluorescent light required for work spaces and do not interfere with interior furnishings or equipment. The neutrals used as a store background color will make it easy to arrange merchandise in color groups without interfering with any merchandise group. Neutrals are basically nonobtrusive and do not clash with any of the color families.

All the design principles that affect the use of texture will be important considerations in composing your display if the neutrals are your dominant color family.

The neutrals used in interiors have been in and out of favor from period to period, century to century, more than any other color family. They are easy to live with, and support the best of the skin tones, the best earth colors, and the best of the wood colors.

The neutrals as used within a composition should appear in amounts of eighty to ninety percent; the remaining color will be the accent colors. The accent color can be varied as much as you like, chosen from any or several color families being harmonious or opposite. Degrees of warmth are of little concern because the neutrals will not evoke strong warm or cool moods. You must balance the neutral color value. Let the light neutral color values dominate, and the dark values added in small amounts provide variety, or vice verse.

The accent colors will establish mood when combined with a dominant neutral color plan, because they are more conspicuous than neutrals. The mood can be changed quickly because the accent colors appear less and can be changed in a composition easier than the dominant color. There are fewer of them, and the accents impact with the neutral family so totally. Accent color distribution in the composition must be carefully balanced because they are conspicuous.

The neutrals are favorite outer apparel colors for fall and winter; they look perfectly natural in the winter landscape. The cityscape remains neutral all year; there is little vegetation to establish the season's mood. The profuse amounts of glass, stone, and other building materials have influenced city dwellers to use the neutral color family as a favorite for their interiors. The moods of a city, the countryside, a resort town or rural village have created certain lifestyles. Each lifestyle has its favorite color family.

The Yellow Family.

Yellow is a warm color. As a rich, light, fragile hue, it is fresh in any combination. The warm variety of the family is red; the cool variety is green. In its grayest value, it remains light in appearance. The color white combined with yellow makes yellow fresher.

Yellow-red grayed is the basic color of some wood and skin tones. Yellow through its orange range is warm and natural. Through its green range, it signals a green, growing image. Yellow-green when used with warm wood and skin tones is best in the avocado variety. Yellow brings out the best and supports the natural colors. The opposite of yellow is blue. The opposite of yellow-green is violet (blue-red); the opposite of yellow-red is blue-green.

Pale or grayed yellow can be used to cover large mass areas because yellow makes less of an imposing color statement than other color families, with the exception of the neutrals. Grayed yellow almost becomes neutral. As long as you can see any yellow in the hue, it remains yellow and should not be considered a neutral. A neutral suggests no color. They are the whites, grays, blacks, and beiges.

The strongest variety of yellow is orange. The redder it gets, the more of a statement it makes. Yellow-red is identified as caution colors. Stripes on highways, warning signs, and caution lights are yellow-red in its brightest intensity. Pastel yellow-red is the parfait or sherbet color. Bright yellow-red is an action color used in resort wear and sportswear (Figure 2-21); darker yellow-red suggests the mellow burnished look of copper and gold. Spring is signalled by the fresh, growing yellow-greens.

Blue absorbs light; yellow reflects light. Yellow becomes light itself. Pale yellow is so fragile that in southern interiors all wood is painted white, including woodwork and chair frames. The darker value of wood is too heavy to be properly balanced with the fragile yellow.

Yellow-orange and orange or yellow-red were combined as fashion interior colors in the sixties. The colors looked great with rosewood, teak, and Scandinavian modern furniture. Later followed pop furniture and Bauhaus, made with new synthetic materials — steel, chrome, and mirrors. Combined with a new lifestyle, both created the popularity of another color family, the neutrals. Gray, white, and mushroom flattered these new materials. The "no color" of the neutrals emphasized the textural quality of the new look, as used by Greta Garbo, the Deusenburg, the Chrysler building lux modern. The yellow-greens and yellow-reds of the sixties related better to the all-wood California style interiors. A product's use and how it fits a lifestyle always influences what color it is to be.

The morning yellows are fragile and sensitive. Mid-day yellows are clean and clear and more active. The evening yellows suggest the patina of antique wood, the richness of brass and copper, the gusto of burning fires.

Many of the great Georgian fabrics, such as the damasks, were woven with combinations of yellow or yellow and white. These colors flattered Honduras mahogany, the favorite wood. They complemented and emphasized the beautifully carved chair frames and cabinets.

The freshness of yellow-green reminds one of lettuce, fern, new willow sprouts. Intense blue and intense red are too heavy to be combined with these colors; they must be used in small amounts. However, pastel red and blue are compatible.

In winter, an intense yellow auto or truck will be very conspicuous. This is because the landscape is very grayed in value, absorbing light. In contrast, the yellow auto or truck reflects light, making it stand out bright and conspicuous.

The Green Family

Green is a cool color. Its warm variety is yellow; its cool variety is blue. The natural greens appearing in nature are yellow-greens. (Figure 2-22) The green-blues generally are related to a product and considered man-made colors. The green-blues are very difficult to use with any warm hues or families. It has always been said that green is a safe, relaxing color for interiors, but green evokes too much of an image to be truly relaxing. Green-blue is the opposite of the yellow-reds, of which brown is an offshoot. These green-blues do not complement the brown of wood tones at all. Red is the opposite of green. Violet or purple (a red-blue) is the opposite of yellow-green. Green-blue is in contrast to skin and food colors. Apparel designers will choose the yellow-greens to work with, as the green-blues are a little harsh with skin colors.

Institutions painted walls green for years, hoping to establish a friendly, relaxed look for the taste of the general public. This did not result. Making things worse, they did not discriminate whether it was a cool variety or a warm variety. Most of us have suffered in waiting rooms being agitated by those greens. The pale yellow family is a safer institutional color because it is quieter. The neutrals are the safest; they can be no-color warm or cool.

Green is the coolest family. Its use in package design symbolizes a cool refreshing product, from lime green, a warm yellow variety, to the coolest mint blue-green.

Green is always identified with the richness of summer. It is somewhat more recessive than blue, followed by red and yellow. The pale greens, both yellow and blue, are favorite summer apparel colors. The pale greens are clean colors. The dark forest greens are favorite winter and fall apparel varieties.

Vegetables are symbolized by the yellow-greens, a good accent color for kitchen products. Green-blue fabrics and wallpapers were favorite decorative elements for the mid-fifties. Forest green was a fashion interior color supporting the Georgian revival furniture. In those updated Georgian rooms, forest green leather covered Chippendale wing chairs. These chairs had frames made of very red mahogany. It was difficult for the designer to stop all these reds and blue-greens from fighting. Lots of wood panelling was used, making the red-yellow of mahogany fight with the green-blue wallpaper or paint. Most of it seemed a bit heavy.

Green is the symbol of grass. Green cork is a good floor material to set the mood of a landscape. The floor plan is where the display arrangement is developed and it establishes a mood. All surfaces in a display or window should be color controlled to help support the major color theme. The floor, walls, and ceiling all contribute to the total color look. These surfaces must be included in your color plan. If green is used on the floor only, one will create a layered look. Green must be repeated on the vertical planes, as well as on the perspective planes.

An abstract landscape display created with geometric symbols need not use realistic color symbols, but a realistic landscape display must conform to certain natural color symbols. The grass could not be bright red or purple. The sky of a display depicting a sunny summer day would not be pink or black. Color image and mood must relate to the effect one is establishing.

Closely related color values on several objects minimize the objects' shape and outline, blurring their impact. The control of color value relationships on merchandise will reinforce the impact of the central merchandise. Objects in the distance are seen as being lighter in value. Very pale colors tend to be atmospheric. A pale color as a background will make that background recede. Likewise, a black wall will seem to come forward. However, if all the space is black, eliminating contrast and definition, the

59

space seems to go on forever. The contour of this space is less defined, and one loses all reference to scale. One has lost the ability to tell where walls meet each other and where they meet the ceiling and floor.

The Color Wheel

To better understand color families and how they relate to each other, it is best to think of them arranged in a circle. This is a color wheel. Figure 2-23 shows the three primary colors. Beginning at the top is yellow, down to the right is blue, and around to the left is red. Figure 2-24 includes the secondary colors between the primary colors. Of course, there are numerous gradations between each color on the wheel. The Grumbacher Color Computer can help you select exactly the right color you want to use in a display. (Figure 2-25).

The neutrals are not shown on the color wheel, but are part of the gray scale. Neutrals result when a color is grayed enough to diminish its impact, producing a beige or gray that has no trace of yellow, green, blue, or red. Value is not illustrated on the color wheel, only hue and intensity. One blue can be made darker or lighter, depending upon the amount of white or black added. This provides hundreds of variations within a color family. Color Composition.

There are many different elements used in creating a display — balance, style, space, line, texture, and form. Color should be used to establish a relationship with these elements. Silk, leather, metal, and wood all are different materials with different textural qualities. If all these elements are red, then red is the cohesive factor. Not all elements in a design should be the same red, but they must be within the same variety of the family. They must also be in the same value range, pastel or dark. At a distance, red vinyl and red velvet will look the same. This provides a common bond. One color family and one variety should dominate by about eighty percent; the remaining color is accent color to be used on small objects. The large dominant objects should fit the dominant color theme. The dominant color should be evenly balanced in the composition, both vertically and horizontally.

Monotony need not be created by using so much of a similar color family and variety. There are hundreds of colors in a range that add to the value changes. The accent color can be an adjacent or opposite color. If too many colors are used, clutter is developed and a weakened image appears. The accent colors must be evenly distributed to establish balance. Balance can be active or static.

The color theme should be directed by the merchandise. The dominant object in the display should establish the dominant color theme. If the central product to be displayed is blue, then blue should be the dominant color in the design. Someone has designed the product using the same basic principles. Repeat the product's accent color. If the dominant blue product has a red stripe on it, then use the red as an accent color. There is no need to develop another theme. Be careful about identifying the product's color variety. Look at it to identify the dominant color sensation, so as not to confuse the warm or cool quality. A white bowl might have a red band on it. White is the dominant color family; it contributes about ninety percent of the color of the bowl. Neutral is the dominant color family to be repeated. Red is the accent color. Red may look like it should be the dominant color because it is the conspicuous one. Red does not contribute enough mass to be dominant; it makes up only ten percent of the color on the bowl.

Many designers make the mistake of repeating an accent color, trying to make it dominant in an interior. It is foolish to choose a yellow sofa to match a tiny yellow buttercup in a painting. Ten paces away you will not see the yellow buttercup. The sofa is large in mass and should fit the dominant color theme of the painting and vice versa. A floral pattern might consist of a range of blue, yellow, green, and brown on a white ground. Often the white ground makes up the greatest percent of color. Do not be confused by the most obvious color. Blue, yellow, green, and brown could be the accent colors.

A product should have the look of one color. This helps impact it. Give it mood and quality. Poorly designed products will have many colors in equal amounts, confusing and blurring its image. This same principle applies to a display. Many colors in equal amounts will create visual confusion.

A display designer must create order in space and he must use color to this end. Color use in the display should be planned with an elevation drawing and rendering. How it is used in volume (three dimensional) will be planned on the floor plan drawing and rendering.

Because neutrals are not color demanding, they are good colors for the walls of a museum and art gallery. The neutrals will not interfere with the collection. One can see that these are good colors for fixtures, carpets, and the walls of a store. The merchandise will begin to impact from all angles if this color palette is used. Monotony can be eliminated by the innovative use of texture. Mirrors, glass, wood, and fabric all have enough textural diversity to make the interior exciting. Intense color should be used in small amounts; it is not necessary to consider repeating these colors in the carpet, as they are accents. The carpet's color must fit in the dominant color scheme. Remember that the neutral is the dominant color family, so any additional color should appear in amounts of only ten to fifteen percent and be evenly distributed as an accent.

When the color palette for the store's interior is developed, the value should be balanced. The darker color values need not all remain at the floor level. These values should be repeated up and down and in and out of the space.

All items for an interior must be chosen with the color theme in mind. The colors of fitting room fabrics, upholstery fabrics, molding hardware, and all supportive materials should be carefully considered so they relate.

All items in a room will contribute color; no detail should exist without color planning and careful color selection.

There is so much multi-colored merchandise on a selling floor that it can all look cluttered. Present the merchandise within color families to create order. Customers will look for the color of an item before any other feature. Customers are beginning to resist wading through groups of merchandise that are presented without color order. Color confusion happens when you cluster items by size. The result is that you have a blue garment next to yellow next to green next to pink and so on...not much of an impression or statement. Hang all garments together within a color family.

Arrange all goods on the selling floor to establish classification, then develop color families. Further arrange the group into fabrics, such as wools and silks. Break it down further into profile, sleeve length, and hem length. Each time the product is split into a group because of classification, fabrication, or profile, you must further position all the merchandise into color groups using the color families as a guide. For example, group all the blue merchandise together next to all the green merchandise, then the red merchandise, and yellow merchandise, followed by the neutral colored merchandise. On one shelf or apparel rack, begin with the darkest of the color families, working into the light color families. If you change classification, the adjacent group must continue into the lightest of the next color family, to the darkest of the next color family, to the lightest until you have created a harmonious rythmn.

If you are working with a group of coordinates, the color breakdown is small. Arranging a group of separates will enable you to mass greater quantities of merchandise. Two hundred and fifty knit tops arranged within color groups allows greater opportunity to fully use the whole color family in arrangement, resulting in a strong impact. If the merchandise is to be folded on a wall unit, start with the top shelf and arrange the color groups top to the bottom shelf. Begin with the blue family, the darkest group, and arange the merchandise in vertical color groups, down to lightest colors in vertical rows until the color range is completed. This arrangement in effect follows the colors as positioned in a rainbow. If products are aligned by color horizontally on each shelf, the color groups get too spread out. A vertical arrangement will better fill the visual range of the customer. Color is the greatest single element to establish an orderly look on the selling floor and back wall.

Colors identify merchandise by season. As fall approaches, move all the pastels and brightly colored summer merchandise to the back of the department. This will enable you to show fresh new dark colored fall arrivals up front, and still develop strong sales with the remaining merchandise impacted in the back. As long as there are substantial quantities of reduced merchandise, continue to arrange it within color groups. You always want to keep the merchandise as highly visible as possible. This is done through color control.

Be careful how the merchandise is lighted on the floor. Fluorescent and vapor lights produce shadowless light. A customer can only see the texture of the product by the way it is lighted. Good lighting can help the textural look of the merchandise, which is one of its best selling points. A dress fabric will shine too much if synthetic and look too flat to be a luxury wool if lighted with shadowless fluorescent light. Fluorescent and quartz lights produce light that is too cool for good color balance, and too glaring to be effective. The cool fluorescent lights will ruin all of the warm colors. The customer's skin tones and makeup will look sallow. Merchandise in a warm color range will lose its richness, becoming grayed, and the merchandise in the red-blue color range will intensify. The cool color families will intensify. Blue-green will become electric. The customer does not live with fluorescent light in his environment. He has incandescent light in his home, and is seen in that light in restaurants. This is the best way to light the merchandise. Incandescent is closer in warmth to daylight and sunshine.

Color memory is short, so do not rely on it. Always work with swatches and color samples. Color reflects from one object to another, forever changing its quality. A white sofa will have a distinct color look, supported by the ambient light and by the furniture surrounding it. Red sofas to its right and left make the white sofa look slightly pink because of light color reflection. The surrounding colors reflecting will create a slight color change of the product. A white sofa may look totally different in another location. It is difficult to move the sofa from place to place. It is easy to move a swatch of that fabric to a new location, checking its color correctness and the effect light has on it in its intended location.

One might spend time selecting paint colors and developing a color scheme for a selling department in the store studio. The light and surrounding materials on location in the selling department will be totally different than the light and color reflection in the studio. To avoid error, check all the color samples on location in the selling department before making your final choice. Lay one color swatch or sample on top of another to see that their relationship is correct. A designer will make a mistake if he goes to one selling department selecting wood products, to another selecting fabric products and to another selecting hardware, hoping that all these colors will be correct for a new location. The quality of light will be different in each parent department, affecting the color of each item selected. To be sure, move the color swatches or color samples from their parent departments to the new selling department location, checking their correct relationship to color reflection and lighting. □

3

Store Lighting

We see objects because of light. We are aware of volume because of light. Mood is created by light. Texture is made obvious or is diminished by light. We compose with light. Light illuminates work areas, allowing overall general visibility. The quality, mood, balance, and nature of color is determined by light. Fine jewelry highlighted in a showcase requires different light than costume jewelry. Meat in a butcher's showcase looks fresh with the proper use of light.

In merchandise presentation, there are two light sources that must be taken into account — electric light and natural sunlight. A designer arranges his interior furnishings around a daylight source to take advantage of natural illumination. In the morning, daylight is fragile and chilly, making colors gray and less intense. Early daylight dramatizes the cool color families. Midday light is strong and better balanced, and colors appear truer. At midday, the intensity of the color is most significant. Late daylight is warm and romantic. Its warmth enhances all the warm color families. Its robust nature makes all colors darker and rich looking.

Electric light must compensate for the lack of daylight. It is also used to balance the quality of daylight. Interiors made chilly by cool, early daylight can be made warm with incandescent light. Natural light intensity can be increased with electric light to compensate for dull winter days and cloudy summer days.

3-1 Z.C.M.I., Salt Lake City UT

3-2 Goldsmith's, Memphis TN

3-3 Gimbels, New York NY

DAYLIGHT

Daylight produces heat as well as light. Draperies are used to control the intrusion of daylight. Stores are designed with fewer windows because it is harder to control daylight. Light changes dramatically and rapidly during the day and from season to season. It is impossible to have clerks constantly opening and closing draperies to control the daylight. It is not practical to have engineers turning lights on and off all day to balance daylight. Also, the merchandise fades if exposed to strong sunlight.

Display windows must be lighted strongly enough so the interior light is brighter than outside daylight to prevent the glare of sunshine on the window glass (Figure 3-2) It is important that light in the display windows has a greater impact than daylight. The display window interiors must be lighted bright enough to make an impact over the store's exterior architecture. The mass of the building, its heavy building materials, design and texture will overpower a poorly lighted display window.

ELECTRIC LIGHT

There are many types of electric lamps available for the designer to use: some portable, some stationary, and some decorative. Neon light is an attention getter. (Figure 3-1) Available in many colors, it is used for its decorative value rather than for its light contribution, which is minimal. Neon light does not generate much heat and will not damage the merchandise.

The workhorse of lighting, the incandescent lightbulb, is called a lamp. Lamps range in size and wattage. They can be enclosed behind a protective shield mounted in the ceiling with a back reflecting material, or fitted with lenses to produce a general non-focused light or a strong spotlight. They can be part of a decorative chandelier or hidden in a cornice.

Clear glass bulbs, when grouped on a wall in a sculptural pattern, produce light and make a decorative statement. Lights arranged in a flat geometric form can suggest endless beautiful patterns. Light arranged in a grid row on a ceiling or on a wall defines space or leads the customer's eye to a specific space.

Lighting fixtures placed on end tables in a shoe department or on counter tops in a cosmetic department add a friendly, decorative light source. (Figure 3-3) Floor spotlights behind a group of plants are enjoyed for their decorative quality and the mood and shadows they create. They provide an additional overall light source. Lamps above mirrors permit the customer to see how she looks in apparel or when trying on makeup. Warm lamps should be used for this kind of lighting. They also provide additional overall general light.

The store is lighted with general light, that is, the light produced by all the lamps in the building. The light level should fit the store's image. Allover bright, glaring light is associated with mass merchandise stores. Exclusive retailers prefer subdued light. Incandescent bulbs produce more heat and burn more electricity than fluorescent tubes. The greater cost for operating incandescent lamps is more than justified by the rich look they give merchandise. Fluorescent lamps produce a shadowless light with an overall glare. In this light, warm colors are destroyed and textures are rendered insignificant. It is wise to combine fluorescent light with daylight and incandescent light to eliminate glare and provide balance.

It is wise to vary light levels. Employees develop eye strain and fatigue working in glare produced by constant general lighting. The employees can move into and out of areas lighted at different levels, enjoying this restful sensation. Eye strain will be reduced, so they will work longer and increase their production. General lighting should produce a variety of light levels. Corridors, aisles, and waiting areas can be lighted with less intensity than the selling floor. The merchandise lighted with greater intensity becomes more conspicuous. Some departments should be more brightly lighted than others. The furniture and shoe departments require less light than the cosmetic department. A change in light levels from one department to another helps customers identify department boundaries.

Perimeter lighting, the light used to illuminate signs, mirrors, cabanas, and walls, adds variety and quality. It must be decorative as well as adequate to light perimeter merchandise. This form of lighting requires built-in or fixed lighting. This lighting will spill over into the department. Perimeter merchandise housed in cabanas must be lighted adequately but not so strongly that it overpowers the merchandise on the floor. Perfect balance must be achieved to create light harmony.

Spotlights at the ceiling or floor level will highlight the merchandise and help to vary light levels. The ceiling spots should be chosen for their flexibility. Since the location of the merchandise on the floor is always changing, the spotlights should be moveable. The lights can be mounted on tracks where they can be easily slipped back and forth, or fitted with clamps that permit them to be quickly moved from one position to another. It is possible to vary the spot bulb color to impact color families. One can vary the wattage or use a general spot or flood type bulb.

The layout for developing proper lighting should be designed on a floor or ceiling plan. Often this plan is referred to as a sight plan. Perimeter lighting should be planned on an elevation drawing. These electrical plans should be clearly drawn to scale, using wiring and fixture symbols.

A ceiling is usually very dull with little design interest, but its contribution to an interior is too significant not to be treated with thought. General light patterns forming monotonous grids can be altered by changing their arrangement. Chandeliers and sculpted light will add interest to the ceiling. Hanging metal or translucent plexi squares or geometric shapes, alternating with light bulbs and repeated at different heights, create beautiful patterns. Nearly all materials can be combined — china, glass, wood, and metal. Vary non-reflective materials with reflective ones. Find new ways of grouping general light on the ceiling. (Figure 3-4) Light grids can be used to vary the ceiling level, some mounted high, others low. If the ceiling levels are varied, use effective lighting to dramatize it. When treated as sculpture, the ceiling will add excitement.

The display must be more brightly lighted than its surroundings in order to be highlighted. (Figure 3-5) The brightness will be determined by the mood of the merchandise. For example, a display of furs will require less brightness than an appliance display. Appliance colors and textures reflect light; the texture and color of fur absorb light. The furs should not be too brightly lighted or it will ruin the look of their soft quality. If the furs are sold as active sportswear, they should be lighted with an allover brightness, as opposed to a stationary elegant fur.

A display window should be lighted with ceiling spots for highlight and add overall backlight to illustrate contour, show the display's depth, and to light the backdrop. Light from the side illustrates the texture of the product and dramatizes the vertical planes, emphasizing the separation of one plane in front of another. The side lights emphasize solid geometric shapes. Side lights are most effective if they are placed at different levels from the floor to the ceiling. Ceiling spots should be arranged at the window proscenium line from left to right and from front to back of the window. The ceiling spots must vary in intensity. Use the brightest lights to highlight the central product and lights of less intensity to illuminate supportive display materials and secondary products. The light must define the space. Do not light the corners of windows or parts of the display that are not to be seen or emphasized. Direct the lights to either expand or reduce the visual field and depth.

Alter the warmth of the spot bulb to emphasize the color mood. Warm red and yellow spot bulbs, alternating with cool green and blue spot bulbs, will make objects look rounder. Combine differently designed ceiling fixtures to do the job. Some spotlight fixtures are designed for varied wattage; others have lenses to focus light and to change color. Some fixtures have light-reflecting and directing panels attached. The fixtures with the brightest spot bulbs should be placed front center and in groups to the extreme right and left. This is major lighting, a ceiling arrangement which requires moveable, flexible fixtures.

The remaining secondary fixtures produce degrees of general lighting to illuminate your composition. Place secondary spotlights on the ceiling front to rear and between the points of major lighting right to left. This is secondary or "fill" light. Side light fixtures should be arranged and grouped to provide secondary light. They are arranged in a vertical row from floor to ceiling at the front of the window. The intense spots grouped at top, middle, and at the floor line is the major side lighting. The lights should be chosen for variation and flexibility. Secondary or fill-in side light should be

3-4 Gaines Mfg. Co., Dallas TX

3-5 O. C. Tanner Co., Salt Lake City UT

grouped between the major light sources.

Neon lamps, table lamps, light sculptures, and decorative fixtures can be combined in the display and arranged with the merchandise for their decorative quality. They also provide an additional light source. (Figures 3-6 and 3-7)

The light plan is inspired by the merchandise, its price, color, texture, shape, size, and mood. Expensive merchandise should be lighted with several spotlights producing the effect that it is lighted from one source. The visual field should be reduced to minimize the importance of supportive elements. To emphasize exclusivity, illustrate the contour of the merchandise with side lights. Emphasize a quality of the contour that expresses its exclusivity. Expensive products are recognized by the rich texture of expensive materials. Well balanced back lighting and side lights will help show this. All the light sources express a quality of color, impacting the mood of the display. Changing the light value of one object in front of another will illustrate its outline or silhouette, creating drama and the uniqueness of each object. (Figure 3-8) Items of similar color and lighted equally will blur the outline, creating less drama. Intense equal light will make you aware of every object in the display. All objects will be seen equally well.

Several small items arranged in a large window look undersized if the window is lighted with equal light intensity. The focus is on the total window. There is a danger that the merchandise will become insignificant in relationship to the total window. Reduce the light and let all the light focus on the objects, thereby diminishing the field of vision and lessening the window size.

Brightly light active windows. Off-balance the lighting to stress tension. Add strobe lights to heighten the activity. Some window displays should be brighter lit in the day than at night to compensate for sun reflecting on the glass, producing glare. Some of the lights should be on timers, turning some lights on and some off to adjust to outside light levels. The level and quality of the light should be adjusted to seasonal changes. Warmer lights in fall and winter support the warm color families of fall merchandise. Darker fall merchandise requires brighter lights to compensate for the dark light-absorbing colors. The pale light-reflecting colors of summer merchandise require less light of the cool variety. Fragile, evenly balanced light creates a light, sensitive mood. Contrasting light levels, creating great shadows, emphasize a heavy, dramatic mood. Shadows will add a pattern effect to your design. (Figure 3-9)

Rooms painted white with light neutrals require less illumination. They reflect light and look bright and airy. Visibility is improved in this space. One can focus on one object or the whole room.

Dark walls, floors, and ceilings are favored by some retailers. This color scheme is synonomous with theater atmosphere. Brightly lighted merchan-

3-6 Rubentein Bros., New Orleans LA

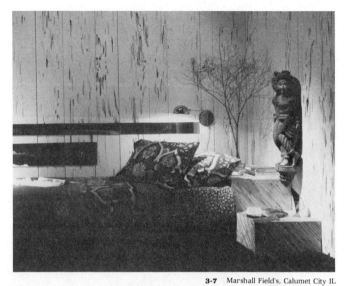

3-7 Marshall Field's, Calumet City IL

3-8 Carson Pirie Scott, Chicago IL

3-9 David Orgell, Beverly Hills CA

dise looks conspicuous in contrast with the dark surroundings. Some small jewelry stores prefer this type of lighting and color balance. A large Eastern retailer painted the whole main floor dark and intensely spotlighted the merchandise to achieve this effect.

The ceiling level is the source of most electric light. A white ceiling looks higher. It reflects light down, producing great illumination with less light, which enhances general lighting. Conversely, dark ceilings make the light source more visible. The ceiling is less conspicuous, absorbs light, and requires more lights to illuminate the space. A dark ceiling looks lower than a white ceiling. Planning ceiling treatment should be part of your overall design.

Most interior light is supplied by ceiling fixtures and is considered "down light." It is important to add "up-lighting" fixtures placed at the floor or near the floor level that project light upward. Light interior displays from below to balance down lighting with up light.

There are many columns in every store interior, and they are often difficult to treat decoratively. Mirrored columns are not too conspicuous, produce a glittering effect and add spaciousness. The use of non-reflective with reflective materials produces an exciting active interplay. Reflected light is strengthened by the use of mirrors.

When light falls on an object, certain wavelengths are absorbed and others are reflected. The reflected wavelengths make up the object's color. A shirt looks red because it reflects red wavelengths and absorbs all other wavelengths. If the red wavelength was missing from the light source, the shirt would have no color but would appear gray. Color is dependent on light source.

When different colored light beams produced by spotlights are mixed, additional varieties are produced. The use of a red and a yellow color filter focused on a white cardboard produce an orange hue. A primary blue spotlight and a primary yellow spotlight focused on a white cardboard produce a green hue. The color filter absorbs all wavelengths except those of the filter's color. Well balanced white light contains all the colors of the spectrum. Sunlight at noon in the summer has a well balanced color distribution. Incandescent lightbulbs produce a light similar to sunlight. Although well balanced, they produce wavelengths that that predominantly in the red family.

Fluorescent light is much different from natural or incandescent light. It produces an uneven color distribution. Warm fluorescent lights produce light that is more intensely red, suppressing green and blue. A cool fluorescent light produces light balanced with the green and blue family, suppressing red and yellow. Fluorescent light produces allover glare. Shadows are eliminated, thus reducing the textural quality of the object. Blues become intense with cool fluorescent light and reds become grayed. Reds become intense with the use of warm fluorescent lights and the blue-greens become grayed. A spot with a red filter will emphasize a red object, making the object look redder. This type of light can be used to light food products; it makes a dining atmosphere pleasant and makes meat look fresh in a butcher shop.

It is important to use well balanced light as produced by the sun. Balanced light color choice is critical. A customer buying a dress or cosmetics has color foremost in her mind, and incandescent light helps her make accurate decisions. It comes closer than any electric light source to producing balanced light. Merchandise lighted with incandescent light helps the customer make critical color choices.

The spotlight fixtures in a display window should be hidden from the customer's view. Front, side, upper, and footlighting should be concealed by prosceniums, lambrequins, and footlight shields. Back light fixtures can be tucked behind the merchandise and decorative panels. Any notice of glare from these lights diminishes the customer's view of the display.

A metal grid suspended from the ceiling of the window will allow you great flexibility in changing the position of spotlights. Spots that can be clamped to this grid will make changing the light arrangement easy and fast. The brightest lights on the upper front sight line should be mounted on tracks and be clipped on bars. They should swivel in all directions for maximum flexibility. Side light fixtures should swivel, as well as move up and down on a track, or be clipped to a pole to make up and down relocation easy.

Electrical outlets must be provided in quantity in the windows and display areas, enabling you to light a decorative lamp in a display or to back light the whole display. You will want to plug in lamps in a lamp display and plug in turntables, light Christmas wreaths and trees. Some china cupboards should be lighted as well as electric appliances. Electrical outlets should be provided to light neon art and other art forms.

Special events and fashion shows need special lighting. The quality of light should be chosen to fit the mood of the event. Spotlights will be needed at the ceiling to both wash the runway and to highlight model pivot locations. Spotlights mounted on the ceiling should be portable and flexible. Footlights must be properly concealed. Lighting that is too strong creates unwanted dramatic lines on the model's body and face. The flowers for the show require less light than the runway but more light than the surrounding ambient light. (Figure 3-10)

Special exhibits must be lighted to dramatize the product and bright enough to separate the exhibit from its surroundings. When you change the light level on a given product or activity by increasing it, you create attention. Special portable light equipment can be rented for special events.

Think of how you would light a mannequin's head. How many lamps used will determine its roundness and mood. One floodlight placed close to the front at eye level produces flat lighting without much modeling. Move

3-10 Z.C.M.I., Salt Lake City UT

the light lower, directing the light up, and you accentuate the eyes and minimize the neck and chin. Move the light high just above the front of the head and you illuminate the forehead and head, as does the light of the sun. Move the light very high and in front of the head and you create deep shadows in the eyes and under the nose. The head looks rounder, but un-flattering shadows are created. Move the light to the side of the head and one side will be in a dramatic shadow, illustrating depth, but only one side of the face will be seen. Move the floodlight behind the head and you see a silhouette against a light background. The contour will be seen clearly but the face will not be visible. Move the floodlight to the front and to one side and the face can be seen clearly but shadows appear along the side of the nose. The lamp's position, either high or low or off to one side, will deter-mine where the top or bottom of the head is lighted. It becomes apparent that more than one lamp is needed.

Two floodlights of the same intensity on either side make an even image of roundness. Move one floodlight back, reducing its intensity and one side of the face looks soft, the other bright and conspicuous. If you cannot move the floodlight back, reduce its wattage. The third dimension looks more natural. We normally see all objects illuminated from all directions and angles. The light source and its reflections make up normal daylight. A third light placed in the background lets the head be seen in relationship to surrounding objects. Additional light above and to each side further illus-trates the roundness of the head. Several lamps both up and down on the side balance the shadows. Many lamps used together produce a nicely bal-anced look of good delineation. There should be a key light source domin-ating, which can be created by one floodlight or by several focused on the same object. The other light should be fill or accent light. Many lights in many positions with varying intensity are needed to achieve a balanced look. How you want to light the item — from the side up or down, front up or down, front to back — determines the lights' positions. A diffused light may help the display mood. This is achieved by shining the spotlamps on a reflective surface and directing the reflected light to illuminate the object.

Your workshop should be lighted with balanced light. It would be nice to have skylights in your studio. Most display work areas are without win-dows, using fluorescent lights to illuminate task areas. Critical color deci-sions must be made. It is important to supply light sources that better reveal color. Combine fluorescent with incandescent light for task areas.

The designer should seek specialized advice for lighting problems. Elec-tricians, light suppliers, power companies, and associated professionals can supply information on the use of their equipment and services. Manufac-turers produce free publications on their products' applications and uses.

The lamp's efficiency is determined by how many watts it has. Lumens refers to the quantity of light given off in all directions. If in one lamp there are 17.5 lumens per watt, a 100 watt bulb produces 1,750 lumens. Another variety of 100 watt bulb may produce 14.9 lumens per watt. The greater the lumens per watt, the shorter the life of the bulb.

Candlepower describes the amount of light given off in a particular direction. Spotlights with lenses are light directing lamps. Knowing the candlepower will help you select the right bulbs for your windows.

The light landing on the object is measured in foot-candles. Foot-candle meters help you measure this. There are equations that determine a minimum for adequate viewing within average work (task) areas. If tasks and conditions are not average, the minimum recommendations will not apply. A dirt filled environment combined with dirt buildup and surface wear will depreciate light. General housekeeping can affect light levels.

$$\frac{\frac{\text{Quality of}}{\text{instruments}} \times \frac{\text{Lamps per}}{\text{instrument}} \times \frac{\text{Lumens}}{\text{per lamp}} \times \text{C.U.} \times \text{M.F.}}{\text{Area of the space in square feet}} = \text{Foot-candles}$$

C.U. is the coefficient of utilization, that is, how many instruments will perform in space of given size with surfaces of given reflectance. Manufacturers supply C.U. ratings for their products. M.F. is the maintenance factor, which describes the depreciation of light created by soil dirt buildup, surface wear and so forth. A maintenance factor of 100 describes a maintenance free instrument.

Foot-lamberts is measured reflection of light from an object. The visual environment is revealed in foot-lamberts.

Designers have available tables that indicate the average reflectance desirable for typical installations. For offices, the ceilings should reflect 80-90; walls, 40-60; furniture, 26-45; office equipment, 25-45; and floors, 20-40 foot-lamberts.

Foot-lambert tables illustrate contrast ratios. Three zones are to be considered as contrast: 1) the task; 2) surface immediately surrounding the task, table or bench; and 3) general surrounding area, floors and walls.

In an office, the task is zone 1 — the desk, table top or bench on which the task is done. Zone 2 — the area surrounding the task — should have foot-lamberts equal to one-third the illumination of zone 1. Zone 3 — the walls and floor — need illumination of only one-fifth that of zone 1. For example, if the task reflects 50 foot-lamberts, the surrounding area should reflect 15 to 20 foot-lamberts, and the walls 10.

The designer must use these tables as reference only. I have taught in many classrooms painted with white ceilings, green walls and evenly distributed fluorescent light of the same warmth, and come away with eye strain and fatigue. The space did fit all the light requirements and all surfaces were prepared to reflect light at the proper ratios, but the overall effect was boring. Let your design skills develop the visual environment and use the Illumination Engineering Society (IES) information as a guide. You must

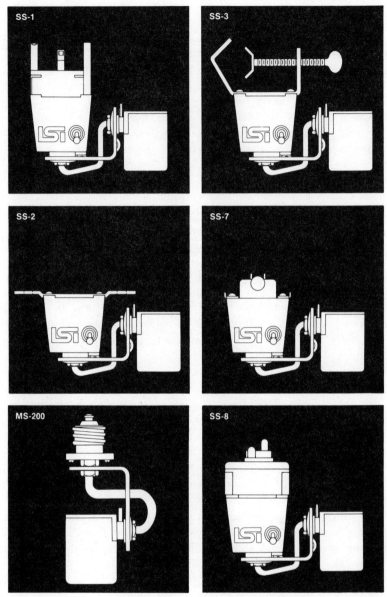

3-11 Lighting Services Inc., New York NY

Swivel fixtures for standard screw-base lamps:
SS-1   With twist-on fitting for lighting track.
SS-2   With universal flange.
SS-3   With C-clamp for pipes, etc.
SS-7, SS-8 With stab-in fitting for lighting track.
MS-200   With male screw plug for standard lamp socket.

interpret quality and mood.

It is necessary to use 12 recessed black can type fixtures, each containing a 250-watt flood bulb, to adequately light 625 square feet. A white reflecting ceiling 14 feet high and general light-absorbing merchandise will improve the light's intensity. The number of fixtures and bulbs can be reduced by 50 percent if the bulb position is moved so that it projects out of the ceiling by a few inches and the can is painted white to reflect the light. The recessed bulb and non-reflecting light fixture impaired the light's value. See Figure 3-11 for examples of different types of spotlight fixtures.

Store management is looking for new high-efficiency lamps that will reduce the cost of general lighting. Metal halide and high-intensity discharge (HID) lamps fit the needs for long life and low wattage. However, their color correction is not well balanced for certain types of merchandising. "Down lights" in the case of HID high sodium vapor and metal halide must be installed in ceilings 13 feet off the floor. Some small shops and boutiques do not have ceilings that are high enough. Exclusive apparel shops where the customer's critical color selection is important cannot use the unbalanced HID or MH lamps. Cosmetic stores also face the problems of producing excellent color balanced light. One other problem about planning allover high intensity general light is that there is less visible distinction between departments and merchandise categories. Filters and methods of diffusing intense glare type lighting reduce the lamp's efficiency. □

4

Tools of
Design

Work space should be provided for each designer. Although an office is not necessary, each designer's space should be divided by low partitions, grouped together and close to a general work area. The cubicles should be equipped with a drawing table, chair, and storage cabinets for staple guns, pins, glue, drawing paper, paint, brushes, scissors, and drawing materials. All the materials that are needed for the day-to-day operation should be close at hand. The cubicles should provide a designer space to plan, make drawings, and file information about schedules, merchandise loan bills, and special projects.

A large general work area (production zone) should be set aside for building props, painting props and rehabilitating display materials. This area should be provided with large work tables. Near this production zone should be stored fabrics, ribbons, drawing papers, cutall tools, small drills, pliers, all kinds of tape, side cutters, wire, glue, and architectural drawings of the store. There should also be an ironing board and steamer for pressing the merchandise. Next to this should be an area for storing mannequins and dressing them.

Mannequins are fixtures, as well as tools for merchandise presentation. They should be stored carefully while not in use. (Figure 4-1) The well dressed mannequin is one of the most important parts of a display. A good supply of additional wigs should be stocked. Mannequins must have makeup applied to fit the category of merchandise they are wearing and

4-1

4-2

hair style that relates to the fashion image. There are sedate poses as well as active ones, so they must be chosen for the fashion mood you are projecting. Active mannequins will be needed for sportswear, elegant mannequins for better apparel. Many mannequins must be stocked to provide you with variety. Age, sex, and pose should vary to provide you with endless possible combinations. Mannequins should be kept fresh looking and be replaced from year to year. Shoes change style often and a mannequin's foot that has been designed for a high heel shoe will not look good or stand properly in a low heeled shoe. Fashion looks demand certain facial and physical types; therefore, new mannequins must be bought to update your collection.

Next to the general work area, there should be a storage area for display materials. One should have a varied collection of flowers, small risers, small fixtures, flooring materials, decorative pottery, and art objects to use in the day-to-day display operation. Included should be a collection of art panels of wood or foam core, with an average size of 4 x 8 feet. Create a collection of panels for ready use ranging in subject matter and style, representing all seasons. Special institutional panels should be stocked for quick access, depicting the store's special sales and events. Many of these art panels are bought from salespersons who call on you two to four times a year. It can be difficult to locate a panel on short notice. Panels should be selected and bought in advance of each season so they are on hand.

The sign shop should be equipped with sign machines that are capable of producing the kind and quantities of signs needed for your store operation. Hand lettered signs will be needed, so a stock of special papers, cardboard, brushes, and paints or inks is essential. Special fonts of type are required for decorative or special sign production. The kinds of letters chosen must reflect in style your store's image and the merchandise. Glue-on letters save time and provide interest, so have a versatile collection of them. (Figure 4-2)

The carpenter shop should include large tables to assist in construction and the assembly of props. Table saws, portable power saws, power staplers and hand saws are essential. Planers and band saws are an additional helpful tool. The carpenter's time is valuable, so supply electrical tools that will help increase his production. (Figure 4-3) A storage area well stocked with lumber should be a part of the shop. Nova ply, plywood, pine-kor and composition board, plus pine 1" x 1" and 2" x 4" boards should be stocked. Electric sanders are a must. Cabinets stocked with screws, nails, and a broad selection of hardware will be helpful.

The paint shop should be supplied with a spray booth, since spraying is the best method of paint application for display materials and fixtures. Compressors are needed to supply air for the professional spray guns and dusting guns. Adequate space should be provided to handle some of the large props and panels that are frequently painted. Storage cabinets must

4-3

be installed to house solvents and a good supply of basic paint colors. Most painters can match and mix any color if they have the basic paints and a good range of color tints. Adequate ventilation systems should be provided for the carpenter and paint shops.

Large shops will need additional warehouse storage for their enormous supply of antiques, decorative materials and props. If the system is large enough, an employee will be needed to spend all of his time storing, shipping and cataloging these props. An office should be set up for this function, so typical office equipment is needed. Trucking systems will be set up to handle the transportation of these materials from store to store. Stores that move teams of display associates from store to store will need to have a van or provide automotive transportation for personnel and display props.

Specially designed small hand trucks and dollies are needed by the display department to move mannequins and props to the selling floors and display windows.

The display manager should have a separate enclosed office for interviewing personnel, talking to vendors, and working out presentation strategies with management. General office equipment is needed. A large presentation table is important for showing moquettes and designs at conferences. Comfortable seating is needed for the conferences he conducts. The display and reference library is often kept in this office.

Some of the display construction work is done in the selling department. Portable tools are needed for this work, as well as for the installation of the displays. Lots of fishing line or transparent wire in varying gauges is needed to fly and hang the display panels from ceilings and prosceniums.

A good supply of spotlights and lighting equipment should always be on hand to provide proper light for the ever changing merchandise mood. A minor supply of electrical hardware and repair materials are needed for this work. Choose pin spotlight fixtures that are low voltage and high intensity. Have a selection of different types of these light fixtures for specific display installations.

Large banks of filing cabinets should be provided for all department accounting records, vendor information, and design research. Special types of file cabinets are needed for large drawings, collateral posters, architectural drawings, and art prints used in displays.

A display department should have a good stock of wrapping papers, wallpapers, and bolts of fabric. Special bins can be purchased or constructed to house this collection in an orderly manner. The fabric collection should consist of felt, cotton, synthetics, vinyl, and velvets in solid colors and patterns ranging from floral to geometric prints. Some trompe l'oeil papers noted for their fool-the-eye designs, fake brick, wood, stone, and marble should be stocked, along with wallpaper in florals, geometrics, and solid textures. The fabrics and papers must represent period designs as well as contemporary designs that vary in styles from cottage prints to sophisticated ones.

All the props purchased, whether they are panels, pottery, or flowers, must represent a variety of seasons, periods, styles, and subject matter. Keep these props in an orderly sequence that represents their design and quality.

Aerosol paints are used for touch up on fixtures and panels. Develop a good collection of basic colors and finishes. Their portability is essential when installing displays. Aerosol paints can be used to touch up damage done in transport or installation in a hurry.

Floor coverings for display windows can be in the form of seamless paper, cork, wood chips, stones, gravel, bricks, wood planks, moss, leaves, shredded metal or paper. Buy and store a collection of these materials in different colors and textures.

Purchase orders, personnel records, typing paper, folders, envelopes, and forms needed for the department's bookkeeping operation should be stocked. They are supplied by the store's supply purchasing department. Inter-store order forms are used to order these supplies.

Paper cutters of varying sizes will assist display designers in trimming papers and are a must for the sign makers to cut correct sign card sizes.

Vellum papers to assist in making architectural drawings, overlays, and for making drawing corrections should be on hand in quantity, as well as watercolor and drawing papers, and poster boards for mounting drawings, signs and illustrations.

T-squares, architectural drawing templates, triangles, scales, and drawing instruments must be available for the many architectural drawings that are needed.

Some display departments do a great deal of silk screening, either for signs or printing decorative designs or messages on large sheets of foam core. A variety of silk screen equipment is available for this. The process saves the design staff time in sign reproduction, and it saves the department money since the designers can create their own decorative panels in lieu of buying them.

There are some large stores that build a great percentage of their own fixtures. A very complete carpenter and paint shop is needed and staffed by a large crew to undertake this type of work. Sometimes these shops are not housed in the store but rather outside, in part of the store's warehouse. A shop of this scale spends part of its time rehabilitating and repairing fixtures. The cost of operation is great and this sort of operation is vanishing. It is being replaced by outside contractors and services.

Apparel stores that do not have their own accessory or shoe departments must keep a large collection of fashionable accessories and hosiery for dressing their mannequins properly. Furniture stores that do not sell decorative home furnishings accessories must invest in and stock a supply of current lamps, china, flower arrangements, art objects, decorative pottery and porcelain to decorate and accessorise furniture groupings. Special draperies, pillows, and bedspreads must be stocked for the furniture displays.

Many table linen and drapery shops must buy special beds and dining tables to display their merchandise. Table linen shops should buy china, silverware, and glassware to make their table settings look fashionable and interesting.

Renting props is a good solution for small shops. Some specialty shops will rent out their merchandise to other stores, so check around for this sort of arrangement. Rental fees are based on a percent of the merchandise price. Advertising agencies, photographic studios, and theaters rent props all the time. They employ stylists whose job is to find the right prop and to rent it for the backdrop of the photo they are working on.

Borrowing items is necessary, even for the complete line department store. A museum collection or collection of rare china is often borrowed for a specific presentation. Borrowing a sports car or boat might be appropriate for the right presentation. Most people respond and lend items with great willingness.

Smocks and special clothing should be provided for the display staff to protect their clothing while doing display tasks. Climbing ladders, lifting display props, and painting display materials can be hard on the associate's personal wardrobe.

An assortment of ladders of varying heights should be on hand to assist the designer in hanging props and for installing displays at overhead heights.

New tools are always being developed to make the display associate's job easier. It is important to buy them when available. □

5

Supply
Sources

After inventory is taken and January's business is complete, the store's profits will be calculated. The annual budget will be determined for the year, including the amount to be spent for signs, mannequins, fixtures, display trim, graphics, and services.

Display suppliers manufacture or sell sign equipment, art supplies, silk screen equipment, mannequins, display trim, graphics, antiques, fixtures, and services. These suppliers are located throughout the world, but most are headquartered here in this country. Most European suppliers have representatives in this country. Suppliers have sales representatives or vendors who call on stores. These salespersons will call at your request or they will make regular calls on a quarterly or semi-annual basis. During these calls, they will show the new lines the suppliers come out with every season. If you want to see these new lines, and you are not a customer of a supplier or if the volume is not large enough to justify a sales call, you can schedule to trip to the supplier's showrooms. Major suppliers have showrooms in Chicago, New York, and on the West Coast. If you have to travel to visit a specific supplier, make it a point to visit all the suppliers in the city. This makes the trip worthwhile. It is wise to make appointments in advance to see suppliers, as some showrooms are open only during certain months.

Every year, there are four trade shows for visual display managers, two in New York and two in San Francisco during spring and fall. These shows

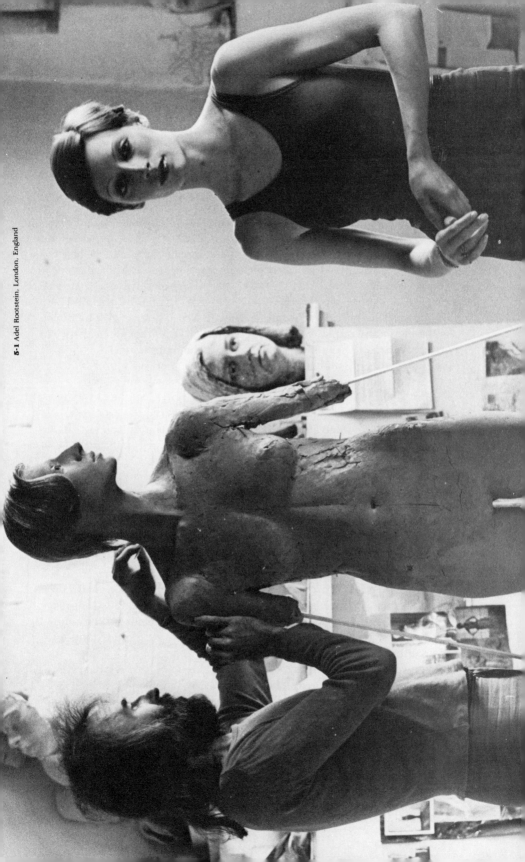

are held in central locations such as hotels or convention centers, making it easy to see many suppliers under one roof. However, in New York all suppliers are not represented at the shows, preferring to have special showings in their showrooms. These showrooms are scattered throughout Manhattan. Be sure to schedule enough time to visit both the show and the showrooms. You never know what special items you might be missing by not covering the entire market.

While you are in large cities, it is important to visit apparel and gift marts. Many suppliers shop these resources, thus adding special decorative items to their lines at a cost greater than you would have paid if you bought them from the mart yourself — avoiding the "middle man." Special baskets, china urns, decorative brass and copper items are found at gift marts. Apparel centers and home furnishings centers show merchandise that your store will stock. It is wise to visit these resources to preview the merchandise. Apparel suppliers on Seventh Avenue in New York are glad to let you see the merchandise that your store purchased. This gives you a chance to correlate special display trim to the "look" of the merchandise.

Country auctions and antique shops provide an endless source of decorative items. Giant gift shows held in major cities are a great source for seeing and buying decorative items. Hundreds of gift manufacturers from throughout the country are represented only at these shows, as their showrooms are too remote to attract buyers. It might take months to visit all the suppliers across the country, whereas it might take only a half a day to visit all of them under one roof at a show.

Great wallpapers and fabrics are available in wholesale furniture, wallpaper, and fabric showrooms. These showrooms are concentrated in large cities and are grouped in furniture marts or in the mart's immediate neighborhood. The Merchandise Mart in Chicago has many floors of furniture, many floors of fabrics, and wallpaper showrooms. It would require several days of taking cabs across cities to see the same resources where the markets are not concentrated.

Seeing these decorative fabrics alerts you to color trends. New drapery and upholstery fabrics might inspire a color palette for one of your displays or promotions. It is wise for a designer to visit home furnishings showrooms at least twice a year to be aware of new trends and to buy wallpapers and fabrics for display uses.

Some vendors specialize in selling artificial flowers and related decorative trim. They sell large pre-made decorative arrangements, individual flowers, and the hardware (wire and materials) to help you assemble your own floral arrangements. Floral vendors have staff designers to insure that the items they have for sale are current with fashion trends. Floral vendors can offer assistance in helping you decide about the quantities, special sizes, and custom work. They can also arrange for special shipping of their products. Floral houses have salespersons who travel in most areas of the country at least twice a year. They will call on you and show you samples and photographs of their materials. It is wise to visit their showrooms to get a firsthand look.

A good working relationship with a local florist is an advantage. Fresh flowers are often needed for special functions and displays. A good florist can get out-of-season flowers, and he can create special floral arrangements for displays. You should select a florist who can develop floral arrangements that are consistent with your tastes and one who has a general understanding of display techniques. Also, make sure the florist you choose can make on-time deliveries. It is a problem to work with any vendor who cannot deliver his merchandise on time, whether it is a shipment of allover store trim or flowers for an event. The time of day deliveries are made is important. Your store's shipping and receiving department has specific working hours, and your staff members have their work schedules. Delivery times should be carefully planned.

Mannequin manufacturers sell their products by three different sales methods: some have their own in-company sales forces; others hire independent sales representatives; and still others sell their mannequins through fixture suppliers. Mannequins can be seen at display shows, in the manufacturer's showrooms, or by appointments with specific salespersons.

Each season, manufacturers produce new lines of mannequins or update old ones. However, some mannequins are classic and require only a change of make-up or hair styles to make them fashionable. There is a wide range of quality between mannequins. Figures 5-1, 5-2, and 5-3 show sculptors creating mannequins from high-fashion models.

Some manufacturers produce costly high-style mannequins, while others produce budget, do-the-job mannequins. The mannequins are such an important presentation tool that great care should be taken with their selection. Durability should not be your only criteria for their choice. The manner in which fashions are worn depends on specific figure types. Always look to vendors who can supply mannequins that can best wear the current fashions. Mannequins are available to make fashion statements for all age groups. You might feel that one manufacturer produces the best male mannequins, another the best juniors mannequins, and still another the best women's fashion mannequins. Therefore, you will probably be buying mannequins from several different vendors. Do not let your budget force you to sacrifice a "look" when you buy mannequins.

Mannequin suppliers sell forms: shirt forms; suit forms; glove forms; and blouse forms. Suit forms are designed with or without pedestals and are placed on display fixtures, cubes, or platforms. Plastic body forms for women's apparel are made in a variety of styles; some have heads and torsos and others just have bodies. They are designed either with floor stands or to sit on counter tops. Some of these forms are abstract and highly stylized, while others are realistic.

93

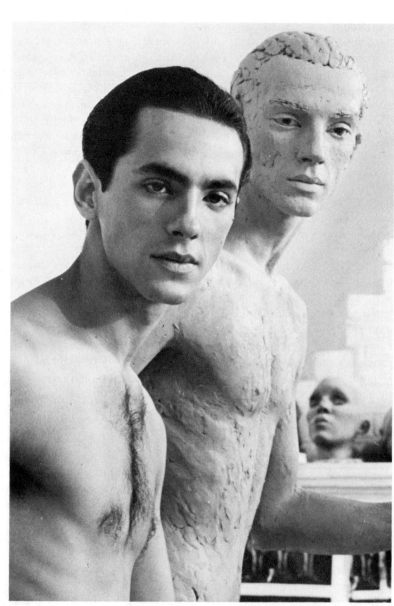

5-2 Adel Rootstein, London, England

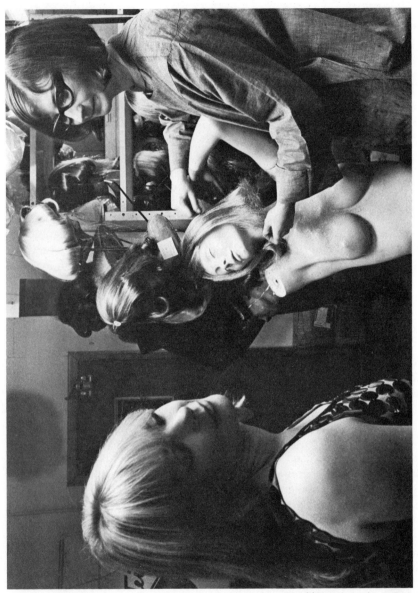

5-3 Adel Rootstein, London, England

Manufacturers can style and make a series of mannequins designed exclusively for your store. They will collaborate to develop a particular face that might be copied from one of your store's favorite models, or they can develop a face that represents a special fashion image. If you need a certain fashion "look" for your windows, custom-made mannequins are certainly worth considering. Manufacturers also rent mannequins. This service is particularly helpful if you are designing a showroom for a trade market. Another service offered by the manufacturers is mannequin repairing. Some independent shops that specialize in mannequin repairs are as skillful as the original manufacturer in making repairs. Generally, the independents are more convenient to the store and they offer pickup and delivery.

Store fixtures can be bought from suppliers who handle everything from sign holders to hosiery forms to lighting equipment. These vendors try to cover as broad a spectrum as possible of fixtures needed by stores. They can create custom fixtures that are made by the manufacturers they represent. But the suppliers are somewhat limited by their design ability and the type of materials used. On the other hand, salespersons who work directly for fixture manufacturers are better qualified to custom make or modify fixtures for you. However, these salespersons offer for sale only the lines of finished products their manufacturers produce.

Some manufacturers do not show completed fixtures in showrooms. They work with store designers and architects to create custom fixtures for new stores. The visual merchandising manager can count on them to produce some small orders, but because of costs they prefer not to. If special fixtures are needed, it is wise to work with manufacturers who can easily modify what they produce. Because of investment spending on the part of the manufacturers, the fixture business has grown by leaps and bounds. A visual merchandising manager will spend more money to buy fixtures than he does for decorative display materials. Good merchandise presentation depends on the appropriate merchandise fixtures. At display shows, the fixture manufacturers far outnumber those who make decorative trim. Some manufacturers of high style fixtures have showrooms only in Chicago and New York. You will have to visit those cities to see their collections. Some fixture suppliers carry a variety of fixture types and send out catalogues describing their lines. Representatives who do not specialize and who carry an assortment of fixtures generally stock those that are fast moving. These supply houses carry hangers, size dividers, some decorative trim, torso forms, sign equipment, hardware, fixtures, and so forth.

Buying fixtures and trim from catalogues saves time, but there is a problem. The manner by which fixtures are photographed tends to highlight their distinctive features and their weaker points are not illustrated. If, for example, you are buying dress racks, it is important to check the welded joints to see that they are clean and strong enough for your purposes.

Check the quality of the plating to see if it meets your standards. Check to see how easily adjustable arms are repositioned, and finally check to determine whether or not the fixtures are strong enough to hold the number of garments you will be placing on them. Color photographs can make cheaply-made decorative trim look better than it is. If at all possible, it is best to personally inspect all the items you intend to buy.

It is important to buy matching fixtures. If you are planning a women's sportswear department, all the T-fixtures, quad racks, and round racks should be of the same design and finish. Be sure the vendor can supply all the fixtures with matching finishes. If you are planning fixtures for a dress salon, be sure you know specifically what merchandise is carried there from season to season. Some fixtures might be too large to house small merchandise classes that are typically housed in a dress salon. The fixtures may not be designed to house some coordinate salon apparel. Count the merchandise and divide it by the number of fixtures that it takes to house the merchandise. Reliable fixture houses will cooperate to provide the appropriate fixtures for your merchandise.

Suppliers who sell decorative trim are the most versatile of all suppliers. These businesses supply flowers, ribbons, decorative panels, decorative wood and metal items, and Christmas ornaments, garlands, and wreathes. They can provide all the items imaginable that are used for props and decorative trim. These vendors sell general decorative and seasonal trim such as Christmas, Easter, Spring, Summer, and Fall trim, ranging from small ornaments to Gothic sized materials for major installations.

Decorative trim items are used a few times, then they are refurbished once or twice and used in a different location before they are discarded. New ideas constantly create the need for new trim. Vendors who carry decorative trim lines call on you many times a year because of the great turnover in trim materials. You must choose decorative trim vendors who can sell exclusive "looks" for your area. Vendors who catalogue mass decorative materials will sell to as many stores as they can. It is a good possibility that the items you buy from them will turn up in your competitor's store in the same shopping center. Buying custom trim guarantees you some degree of exclusivity. Vendors who sell top lines will provide the names of the local stores that have bought their products, or they will not show you items that have been sold to the competition in the neighborhood. Custom items will cost slightly more, but they are worth it since you do not have to worry about seeing the trim in other stores. On the other hand, visual merchandising managers might not buy exclusive trim. They use inexpensive trim items to fabricate decorative trim of their own design.

After you have done business with vendors for a period of time, you soon learn which vendors have the right trim and which vendors can best work to supply the correct "look" for your store. Also, vendors and manufacturers become aware of the work you do and they are able to create special items with very little communication. At this point, the designer and the vendor can begin to collaborate with great understanding and sensitivity. Manufacturers who comprehend your sense of design can make special trim even when they work from the simplest sketches and color samples. This saves the time spent having to check on a manufacturer's production and design progress.

You never know where you are going to find display materials. For example, they can be found at a lumber yard. A different kind of building material handled in a special way as a prop may solve a display problem. Gift shows and gift markets provide a never ending source of materials. A bale of hay or one hundred pounds of grain used as floor covering can make the local feed store a resource. It is important to always be on the lookout for stores, vendors, and manufacturers who might carry new products for display materials. Above all, watch for special trim items carried in your store. China, flowers, fine art, glass, lamps, fabrics, papers, pillows, furniture, and gift items in stock can be used as decorative display props.

Display houses show their Christmas lines in June and their Spring lines in November. Always look for trim well in advance of the date you plan to use it. Some of the items will be purchased as they appear in the line, others will require modification, and still others will be custom made. This advanced buying gives adequate time to plan the trim and gives the vendors adequate time to produce the trim. If you wait until the last minute, you might be forced to accept substitutions from the materials the vendors have left in stock or only what the vendors have time to produce and ship.

Always look at important vendors' lines even though you may have no budget to buy anything. Take notes of the items you want to buy later, when the budget is available. When you have money to spend, the vendor might not be available. Some of the best vendors work out of New York City and call on stores periodically. Therefore, it is best to consider all the items in a vendor's line because you never know when a special need might arise for a particular item. Remember that buying items from vendors is not as simple as running down to a store and picking out whatever you want. Most vendors are knowledgeable enough to let a display person see their lines, even though they know there is no immediate sale. They realize that future sales are possible.

When you buy from a vendor, he will write a sales order for the items you want. This will be confirmed with a purchase order from your store. Be sure that both you and the vendor understand the purchase. Make sure all line numbers and quantities are correct. Confirm specific shipping and receiving dates. Make sure you include any favorable discounts. Spell out payment terms and discounts. Be sure you understand whether you pay any or all the freight from their warehouse or a consolidation point. Understand the vendor's return and cancellation policies.

Some display vendors offer special services such as refurbishing your old trim for another season's use or finding buyers for your used, unwanted trim. Some vendors subcontract items that they do not produce. If a major trim is planned and the vendor does not sell a special matching tablecloth, he will have one made by one of his subcontractors. If your major trim includes a metal arch and the vendor does not produce metal arches, he will have the work subcontracted. When one vendor is supplying most of your major trim, be sure to ask him about the special subcontract services he offers. If your order is large enough, the vendor will handle additional work with very effective cost results.

Many display houses have their own designers who can be very helpful in modifying or perfecting your designs for custom props. They supply this service for no added costs. Some vendors who handle major seasonal trim for shopping plazas will handle its installation and removal. In some large cities, there are display houses that will sell you all the Christmas display trim components and then install and remove them. If your store has a small staff, the installation and removal costs might be justifiable.

There are many display companies that specialize in producing only graphic panels. These silkscreened panels can be decorative or in the form of stylized signs. The companies can produce any special designs, photos, and flat pattern designs of any subject in any color. They also have stock panels or they will make custom panels using your designs. Additionally, the companies have their own designers who can take your ideas and turn them into completed designs. The panels cover large areas at little cost and they produce stunning sophisticated effects. Some of the panels approach the level of fine art. Panels are great for creating backgrounds for windows and interior displays. Not all display houses specialize in selling panels, but they carry them in their line. The panels are printed by graphic houses and sold in large quantities to vendors, or the vendors will subcontract the printing of a limited number of panels. These panels might be part of a flower or prop line the vendors carry. The visual merchandising manager must be careful when buying panels from non-specialists because they are cheaply printed in quantities that reduce their exclusivity.

There are a number of manufacturers in the Orient who produce inexpensive items for the display market. They have flooded the market with plastic plants, fish, birds, raffia items, and paper items. If you see five vendors and all five carry the same items, you can be sure they are selling these items to every store. When you see the same paper sunburst in a dozen different stores, you wonder about the creative level and selectivity of the visual merchandising designer.

When you need a decorative display item, you must determine whether it is more cost effective to buy the item or have it produced by your staff. With the trend toward smaller display staffs and higher labor costs, it might be cheaper to buy the item. Stores that have large budgets, central buying systems, and special production teams might find it cheaper to make specific display items themselves.

Show card machines and type faces are sold by show card companies. These machines are produced to print up to 22" x 28" signs and 15" x 45" banners. Stores that need a great variety of signs in all sizes prefer the 22" x 28" production machine. The standard size card stock is 22" x 28". All sign sizes 22" x 28", 14" x 22", 11" x 14", 7" x 11", and 5½" x 7" can be cut from a 22" x 28" card without waste. Manufacturers of sign holders produce them in sizes that correspond to the basic card sizes. Inks, type cleaners, spacers, and other supplies are also sold by the sign machine companies. Your sign requirements will determine the size and quality of the printing machine you need. Drying racks, paper cutters, and special work tables should be considered when you plan to purchase a show card machine.

Silk screen equipment for printing signs is supplied by silk screen manufacturers. The screens can be very small and simple or they can be large and complex. Large equipment that is able to print signs and decorative panels is produced with accompanying photographic equipment to allow you to make screens from large photo blowups. The silk screen manufacturers also produce related supplies and equipment.

Some companies make letters of molded plastic, plexiglas, and styrofoam. These letters are made of almost any conceivable materials in all sizes and type styles. The letters are either applied to surfaces or self standing. They can be used to make traditional signs or more dramatic graphic art statements. The use of individual letters provides the designer with great flexibility and freedom in his layout. The letters can be applied to any material or surface. Mounted on a wall or lying flat on a floor of a window, these letters produce instant signs. The use of these letters is decorative and for the most part they are not used as merchandise signs.

Art stores, located in every town, are great sources of special drawing papers, watercolor papers, drafting equipment, and drawing tools. Inks, paint, and art papers should always be well stocked in your department. Hobby stores are a source for special tapes, glues, and assorted ribbon trims.

The best sources for lighting equipment are: electrical supply houses; electrical contractors; light fixture supply houses; and some display houses. Theatrical light fixtures and equipment can be found at companies which specialize in such fixtures. Some display vendors carry a limited stock of theatrical lighting equipment. Large electrical suppliers sell everything from spot bulbs to wiring to outlets. The suppliers produce enormous catalogues. Pore through these books and familiarize yourself with their contents. This will probably give you many ideas about using lighting in your displays.

Special hardware is always needed by the visual merchandising designer. However, all the hardware needed is not available at local hardware stores. It must come from large commercial hardware suppliers who carry unique hardware items. These suppliers also distribute comprehensive catalogues listing their wares. It is wise to become familiar with their stock.

Paint and lumber are used in large quantities by visual merchandising departments. Find a paint source that can supply custom colors mixed for you in large batches. Try to always be aware of new products as they are introduced to paint and lumber dealers.

Local suppliers of tools and spray equipment will help you equip your shop with saws, cut-all equipment, power staplers, and hand tools. Paint spray equipment, from compressors to spray guns and parts, are available from the manufacturers of paint spray equipment. Their salespersons will help you plan, set up, and inform you about the use of spray equipment.

Since your displays are created by the assemblage and use of all the materials outlined in this chapter, it is important that you keep updated about them at all times. □

6

The
Merchandise

It is not difficult to imagine how to create a display if you let the merchandise be your guide. For example, when developing a shoe display, let the color and shape of the shoe give you clues for display colors and patterns. (Figure 6-1) Shoe texture helps you select related materials, whether they are smooth, shiny, or rough. The shoe category and style determines whether the display is casual or sophisticated. The display location (in the store window, front of the shoe department, or with related fashion items) is dictated by the buyer's plans for the shoe, that is, whether the shoe is promotional, for a sale, a basic stock shoe, or a fashion item.

The VM designer cannot function without merchandise nor can he function effectively without understanding the place of the merchandise in the overall marketing scheme. To gain this knowledge, he must communicate with members of the merchandising group, fashion staff, and advertising department. They will keep him informed about merchandising policies and tactics with which he can design displays that tie-in with and complement the store's total selling effort. It is worth noting that large department stores have separate departments for each of the above groups; however, in smaller stores the designer may be responsible for one or more of these functions. Whatever the case, it takes a collaboration of ideas to make the greatest sales impact.

The buyer is responsible for the merchandise. Frequently though, the VM designer will help the buyer select fashion merchandise at market.

6-1 Z.C.M.I., Salt Lake City UT

6-2 Marshall Field's, Calumet City IL

Their selection is based upon the item of merchandise, the item's category and how it will be presented in the store, its advertising value, display location requirements, and the fixtures upon which the item will be presented. Normally, the buyer is limited to the merchandise shown at the market and his budget. Other factors that affect his purchasing decisions are advertising campaigns, store promotions, seasonal requirements, and fashion trends. Of course, all the buyer's purchases must be in keeping with his store's market and image.

If you do not help the buyer select the merchandise, you must get him to show you the fashion styles he bought. This is an on-going process, as styles change monthly, semi-annually, and annually. Fashion displays change more frequently than non-fashion displays. For any given period, your store will commit itself to one or two styles and it's your responsibility as VM designer to be familiar with them so you can plan your displays to promote and present the styles in the most salable manner possible.

There are only so many manufacturers who produce merchandise in the quantity, quality, and style to supply your type of store. Therefore, many stores in the same class (yours and your competitor's) catering to the same market will offer the same merchandise. The VM designer must rely upon store theater and product presentation to make the merchandise appear unique and desirable and, above all, make it salable.

Many publications specialize in the fashion industry. They prepare and illustrate articles about fashion trends. These magazines are a good source of information to help you select the fashion trends that are most compatible with your store's image and merchandise. You do not set fashion trends; you create display trends.

There is a great amount of information available to the VM designer about the merchandise his store purchased. This information is obtained from the merchandising group and fashion staff in the form of memos and video tapes. You, the designer, must translate this data into good merchandise presentations that reinforce the established fashion trends. Speaking of presentations, studies show that all shoppers are more influenced by fashions displayed on mannequins than displayed in fashion shows or illustrated in advertisements. (Figure 6-2)

Large department stores set aside part of their budget to buy merchandise for special displays. What is purchased is usually the result of ideas from the merchandising, advertising, fashion, special events, and VM staffs. These special displays are designed to generate store fashion trends.

Before the visual merchandiser selects props or display materials, he must be totally aware of his store's merchandise program. Obviously, the selection of items must be geared to the program. It takes well co-ordinated advance planning to accomplish this purpose. Believe it or not, many VM designers make the mistake of buying props to project a fashion image that is not related to their store's merchandise.

6-3 J. L. Hudson, Kalamazoo MI

Do not overlook technological advances when planning merchandise presentations. New threads, colors, and shapes can have a vital influence upon your choice of colors and materials used in a display and enhance a rather run-of-the-mill presentation. The pattern of a dress can be repeated in a background prop and a part of the design can be used in a piece of furniture or other related product.

It is important to note that merchandise manufacturers are very sensitive to fashion trends, particularly color trends, and they produce items using new colors. You will find the producers use these colors in the creation of furniture, fabrics, shoes, appliances, haute couture, ready-to-wear, and many other items. Therefore, it is easy to assemble a presentation based upon combinations of these products and colors. Further assistance comes from the display manufacturers who provide materials using the current colors. It is apparent why a Lagerfield dress looks great with Art Deco and Bauhaus furniture. All these items have color and design similarities.

Customer life styles often inspire the creation of new products . . . a good example is active sportswear. When this product was developed, the stores had to adapt to its market impact. New departments were established to house and sell the sportswear. These shops were decorated with bright, T-shirt colors. Clear, simple display shapes were used to accentuate the clothing profile. Manufacturers responded with a wide variety of accessories and clothing based upon the sportswear design principles. New display fixtures, mannequins, and materials were created to support the "look." (Figure 6-3)

To take full advantage of this merchandise trend, the VM designer had to be totally aware of its direction so he could be selective enough with his choice of displays to maximize the effect of his clothing presentation. Historically, it is interesting to look back to a period and see how architecture, products, and fine arts all had similar color and design characteristics, all relating to a particular culture and a life style.

Stores develop sales promotions around life styles and products. These events are institutional and storewide and generally they last for a period of two weeks or longer. A brief profile of such a promotion is described in the following paragraphs.

Management decides the economic forecasts for a future month indicate that sales will be less than expected. Obviously, a special effort is required to prevent the store's sales income from slipping below normal expectations. Therefore, more emphasis will be placed upon sales, advertising, promotion, and merchandise presentation. To do this, management establishes a concept "Britannia" as a store-wide theme to generate traffic and build sales through the anticipated slow period.

Buyers are notified about the theme and are given budgets to buy merchandise for the promotion. They go to the market and seek products that

6-4 Woodward, Calgary, Alberta

6-5 Thelma Stannard, New York NY

pertain to the store's customers, the season, and the event. The fashion and VM directors help the buyers select the best looking merchandise. After the goods are purchased and the delivery dates confirmed, advertising and VM meetings are held to determine strategies.

Management, which includes the VM director, decides which departments can best handle the event and whether or not outposts and special shops should be set up. (Figure 6-4) Key merchandise is reviewed to determine the items that go into a window, an advertisement, a fashion show and what items should be prominently displayed. The VM director decides what special fixtures, props, mannequins, and materials are needed to support the event.

The buyer contacts manufacturers to see if they can supply informal models, fashion presentations, and product demonstrations for the event. The manufacturers usually have funds, package shows, signs, or fixtures available to help with the promotion of their products. (Figure 6-5) The VM designer should be very discriminating when selecting sales aids from manufacturers, as some will complement the store's promotion and others will not. The VM department supplies all the fixtures and materials to make the events workable. These can include fashion show runways, special lighting, sound systems, special effects, and personnel to produce the show. Store shops are rearranged to accommodate merchandise in central groups.

The VM director decides the visual theme to be used for the event and in this instance he chooses red, white, and blue colors with stars as the design symbols. All the displays in the store will repeat this theme. Plans are made early for building and buying props and for incorporating the design symbols and colors on shopping bags, wrapping paper, mailers, catalog covers, and in advertising.

You, the designer, are expected to formulate other ideas for the event. For example, you might use an antique automobile in the store. The restaurant can serve special foods, be decorated accordingly, and have special theme music. In-store celebrity appearances by designers, authors, artists, musicians, and craftsmen can enhance many events. You will set up special displays to announce and support these appearances. Displays featuring vendors preparing foods in the small appliances deapartment are very effective. If crowd control is deemed necessary, you will make arrangements for any control equipment that may be needed.

Flags, banners, bunting, and graphics are considered capable of producing the best institutional look for the event. They are large enough to provide coverage and be extremely visible. Smaller versions of these props are used for in-department displays. The more the design idea is repeated, the more effective is the message. Plans for special flowers are made in advance.

Place all red, white, and blue merchandise on mannequins and group the mannequins toward the front of the departments. Use other British merchandise with feature displays instead of props. Merchandise impact on customers will be better if you style it. Base your presentation on the following steps: merchandise category, classification, subclassification, fabrication, color, price, and size.

A great many signs are needed for a store-wide event. The signs should have a headline repeating the design colors and theme. Some signs describe the merchandise and its prices, other identify and describe the event. Do not overlook the lead time needed to produce signs.

As the theme grows, more vendors will offer special promotions and store theater "happenings." Some promotions will be developed by the store such as dance lessons, soft drink parties, and cosmetic make-up lessons. Remember, all promotions regardless of their source are produced and staged by the VM designer. A successful event can boost store sales by eight or ten percentage points.

The selection of props can make or break a merchandise presentation. Never, but never, find a good looking prop and decide to build a display around it. Keep things in perspective when designing a display and above all, remember the purpose of the display. Start with the merchandise. You will find that the ideas will come easier, execution of the design will be simpler, and the display will have more meaning. Consider this basic example: a very effective presentation can be made by using all red T-shirts. Hang them on a round rack, a waterfall T-rack, or on a quad rack and place them in an obvious spot at the front of a department. This impacts the merchandise classification.

If you display a group of easy, slouch, red shirts, think about all the things they remind you of — soft sculpture, easy unstructured furniture, and soft edge graphics. All these items can be used as props to complement the shirts. Every time you repeat the shirt color or design, you make the shirts look more significant. Four shirts appear more important than one. Unrelated colors or shapes create clutter.

Department stores have a complete line of merchandise and it is all available to the VM designer. If a painting is needed for a prop, it can be obtained from the art gallery. Furniture, lamps, crystal, and china can be used as props in any location in the store. However, small stores and specialty shops do not have a wide variety of merchandise. If a painting or sofa is needed, it must be purchased. Because of the costs, these kinds of props are very seldom seen in small stores. Specialty shop VM designers rely on display props and it is easy to see why they started the "bare minimum" display trend where few props are used. In some instances and for no apparent reason, some department stores follow this trend.

A few department store merchandise executives suggest the pure minimum look is best. They forget they have an opportunity to work with great and varied collections of merchandise. Some of them believe that a shoe presentation should not be combined with other merchandise. However, if a scarf or purse makes a shoe look great, they should be used as they make the display less boring and there is a good chance all the items will be sold.

Grocers have been piling one product ceiling-high forever. A customer does identify with the product in this instance, but the specialty and department stores are another kind of retailer, and generally "piling on" in these businesses can be very tedious. Of course, display philosophies will be enunciated by divisional managers; some have ideas about how the merchandise should be presented, while others recognize your expertise and leave the presentations up to you.

Sales patterns dictate how many windows and displays you assign to a particular product. It is easier to present a best seller than it is to promote a poor producer. If you create interest in a best seller you might increase sales by ten percent of an anticipated $100,000 gross. That is more desirable than a ten percent increase in a loser with a $25,000 gross. □

7

Budgetary Concerns

The store manager will ask you to prepare next year's display budget request and submit it at least one quarter before the beginning of the new fiscal year. He will make suggestions about how much money can be spent in the new year. After a critical evaluation of the past twelve months, develop a preliminary budget and give it to the store manager for approval. If you think more money is required, you must give a logical, reasonable explanation to justify the expenditure. You must establish that the money requested will directly generate sales based upon improvements you have planned. The investment must be cost effective. The store manager then submits the budget to the company president for approval. The manager must be prepared to explain why you are requesting additional funds. He must understand the reasons behind your budget requests for payroll, display materials, and capitalized display materials. The budget should be broken down into months and quarters to help you determine expenses by season and month.

The Christmas season requires the greatest portion of the budget. The windows are more lavishly decorated and the interiors are more completely decorated than at any other time. (Figure 7-1) The cost of materials is greater and it takes a larger staff to execute and install the displays. The first group of Christmas shops are installed in October. The major trim must be installed the first week in November and the windows open that same week. The activity takes fifty percent or more of your budget which is allocated for the months of October and November.

7-1 Z.C.M.I., Salt Lake City UT

It is important to review last year's budget to see how much money was spent and how effectively it was spent. Check to determine whether you were over or under budget and whether or not the correct amounts of money were allocated to the proper months. Review the monthly amounts and determine if enough money is budgeted for the various months. For example, the date for Easter changes every year and you must make sure that money for Easter displays is budgeted for the proper month. If you plan to have special displays made, they are sometimes fabricated a month in advance of the display installation; therefore, you must have money budgeted for the month of their arrival. Some materials for a display must be ordered two months in advance of the display installation date, so you must be sure to adjust your budget for the arrival of these materials. Keep in mind that the arrival of materials does not always coincide with their installation dates. Reserve money for the cost of the display's installation. Some seasonal displays have their costs factored over a three month period (such as Christmas). Some displays are made and installed in the same month which allows you to budget the entire cost of the display in that month. For example, daily operations and weekly window changes fall into this category.

The annual budget should be reviewed in December, which allows you to evaluate the current Christmas look. It is wise to think about salvaging the most effective materials for use next year. You can determine what can be added, deleted and what needs to be refurbished. Calculate the cost. If you think more money is needed for next Christmas and you doubt if the budget will be increased, you can move some of the money from June or July, a less active period, to October or November.

Each year the costs of materials and labor increases. Determine the rate of inflation and add it to your budget. If the budget cannot be increased, you can move money from the slow months to the months that require the greatest expenditures. Plan the payroll to include pay increases for your staff. It might be necessary to adjust the number of your staff members to compensate for the pay raises which increase the payroll costs. The time for salary increases for your employees varies from month to month. These costs grow and can be at maximum in the last quarter.

Capital expenditures include the cost of mannequins, fixtures, and remodelling. These expenditures are deducted from taxes at a different rate than daily operating costs and materials. A separate budget is set up to account for these costs. For your capital materials budget, determine when you will need new mannequins for replacement or new mannequins designed to project a new fashion look. Perhaps new fixtures are needed for a special Christmas shop or to house new merchandise arrivals. Set aside capital funds in the proper month for these expenditures. Determine what remodelling or refurbishing is required and the months in which it will be accomplished. Consider all the costs for the upcoming year. Estimate the amounts and when they will occur.

Budgets are based on the store's annual sales and operating costs. Profits and losses will determine how much you can spend. Budgets are adjusted monthly and quarterly to reflect the sales, profits, and losses. Sales may be increasing dramatically but if the costs are too great, they must be pared to balance the ratio for profitability. The budget is a percentage of the profitable sales. Greater budgets will be provided if you continue to make the store's presentation exciting, so the merchandise will look desirable, thereby increasing traffic and sales. Should the budget be reduced, you must buy only the important display materials for the important selling seasons, and expenditures must be cost effective. Buy mannequins and fixtures and invest in good help. Buy very few trend materials. Display materials can be rehabilitated by using them in new locations, in different combinations or repainting them. This will save considerable money.

When preparing a budget, assign all anticipated expenditures to the correct month and the correct category — operating, display, or capital costs.

A. Operating costs. Salaries for freelance workers, consultants, special labor, carpenters, painters, and workmen for special installations are controlled by a cost budget. Special services including seamstresses to make special draperies and press and alter apparel for the mannequins; electricians to create special lighting, etc. Although they are on salaries, they do not fit in your payroll budget.

B. Display costs. Decorative papers, decorative panels, tools, antiques, accessories, pottery, floor covering materials, fabric, ribbon supplies, Christmas wreathes and garlands, light fixtures and lighting equipment, decorative cubes, animals, animated figures, foliage and flowers, and any item that is purchased or rented as a prop. Additional items are signs, paper, ink, sign equipment and tools, are grouped in the display cost budget.

C. Capital costs. The purchase of mannequins, fixtures, their repair, refinishing, and modification, remodelling costs, carpet, paint and electrical work, furniture, wallpaper and fabric are all capital costs.

The budget should be reviewed and adjusted every month. New events, shops, new emphasis on a merchandise category, unforeseen repairs, and special sales campaigns will add to the cost of a month. These costs may not have been anticipated or perhaps they are newly created. If you do not want to go over budget, increase or decrease the balance amounts from month to month but stay balanced within the quarter. If you spend too far in advance, you will lose control and you might never find money to balance the accounting of the past month's overspending. The costs should be separated into two categories: those that reflect advanced costs, and those that reflect day-to-day costs.

Have a display props sale. This will generate new money for you. The store customers love these sales. You might contact a friendly competitor to buy last year's Christmas trim or other display materials, mannequins, and fixtures that are no longer needed. The buying company will be billed by you on an invoice. The check for payment can be sent to you. You will forward the check to accounts receivable and they will in turn credit your account.

Develop a system for recording each purchase and each charge for the month. Record the amount, date, and purchase order number for each expenditure in a ledger. File the corresponding purchase orders by the same month. Deduct the amount of each entry (expenditure) from the amount of your budget. Deduct and record shipping costs. Insist that display materials are received in the month that you have budgeted. You hope that materials ordered for March delivery are received and paid for in March. Remind suppliers to invoice the materials with receivables so the bills can promptly be paid for in the proper month and that any discounts for prompt payment are taken advantage of. It is difficult to pay for merchandise received and billed in May when you budgeted for it in March. Remember to include costs of services, supplies and so forth. Although you can readjust the budget month to month by decreasing or increasing it, you must be within the budget at quarter and year ends.

Review the budget from day to day, making plans for the effective use of the balance to compensate for future charges. Refer to your purchase orders to determine what deliveries are expected in the future. Make budget critique notes about costs and reasons for over or under spending. This information will help you evaluate deviations and set strategies for next year. Next year, you can refer to these notes to determine the reason for peaks in spending.

A purchase order must be written for each purchase or charge. Each account that you are responsible for will have an account number for each of the following: payroll; display; expense; and capital. The use of account numbers helps you get the charges in the right spot. Each budget is identified by an account number.

It is important to fill out purchase orders accurately. List the vendor's name, where you want the goods shipped and on what carrier and the delivery date and terms. Describe the merchandise by style, number, and color. Note quantity and price. The purchase order must have the account number and your department number so accounting will apply it to the correct account and department. The purchase order establishes the receipt and payment document cycle.

A purchase order consists of four copies. One is a vendor's copy that is given to his salesperson or sent to the supplier. It is used by the vendor to fill the order and get it shipped to you. The information on the vendor's copy will enable him to invoice or bill you. The purchase order is the document accounts payable uses for paying the vendor. The receiving copy of the purchase order will be in the hands of the shipping and receiving department. Their copy will allow them to count and check the order properly. Quantities received and damaged materials are recorded at this point. The accounting department, after all goods are in and accounted for, will match the invoice with the purchase order and pay the vendor. The section copy will be your reference for the whole transaction. The purchase order will be the official record of each purchase. It is used for all store purchases by all buying agents.

Daily time records must be kept for your staff, including the hours and days that they have worked. The store will supply you with these record forms. Proper record keeping enables you to see if you are conforming with the payroll budget.

Weekly work schedules must be typed for your staff. This will allow you to schedule and budget their time for each project and to meet deadlines. The schedule can be modified at morning meetings to adjust for new projects and to evaluate the progress of existing projects.

Small inexpensive items must be purchased. Not all retailers accept purchase orders. Petty cash is available for paying for these supplies. Petty cash amounts received are charged to your budget.

Merchandise in your store that is purchased by you for display will be charged to your budget. Goods are billed to you at cost plus shipping charges. In a full-line department store, supplies, fabrics, and decorative items can be bought at a price that will help your budget. These charges can build up quickly. They must be recorded daily on your expense ledger. It is a good practice to keep the store manager informed at all times about your budget, budget goals and any problems you might be having with the budget.

The cost of your buying trips will be paid for by the store but will come from the company's travel budget. Local travel is charged to a general store account.

Advertising schedules and events schedules must be kept and referred to each day to make sure displays and signs are created for them. You must type window and feature display schedules for the merchandise group. They must have the merchandise ready for your display well in advance.

You must record the location of the merchandise displayed in a store for the merchant's benefit. He must be aware of its location for inventory control. Also, if a customer wants a product on display, the merchant can refer to the list making it easy to find.

Record information about key displays of the past year. Evaluate the display. Note its effectiveness and weakness. Make notes on the time of installation, duration, its impact, and its cost. File floor plans, drawings, and photographs of the display. This reference will be invaluable for the staff in establishing new ideas about future displays. It will be a good reference for management to evaluate the importance of the display and its location. It will help management determine quantities of merchandise to support the display or event next year.

A file of technical information should be kept for reference. Floor plans of the store are referred to daily. They must be kept current, reflecting remodelling and department relocations. A file of pamphlets and catalogues from vendors, illustrating display materials, fixtures, mannequins, supplies, and hardware must be maintained for quick reference. It is always good to know who makes what and where to find it. Lists of key suppliers and their phone numbers are helpful.

A library of trade publications and books will help you research new ideas for displays. Back issues of *Visual Merchandising* magazine should be reviewed to see how other designers have solved their problems.

File employee records. They record current salaries and personal information; they are a great help at employee review time. Employee goals should be noted on these records. With this information you can help guide the employee to arrive at these goals and stay on track.

Display materials stored in a warehouse must be recorded. A description and photo must be kept for reference. Getting to and into the warehouse can be time consuming; therefore, accurate complete files must be kept. Large department stores employ a staff to record information about warehoused display materials.

The store publishes daily sales and monthly inventory reports. Sales are published by the store, department, and group. Reports comparing sales against the day and the month and the year are available. There are reports covering every aspect of sales. This information is not available to all employees and is confidential. It is filed in a central location. You must analyze these figures and determine if the presentation in a department is either weak or strong and how it is affecting sales. If you have the solution to increase sales by better presentation, then you must alert management. Sales figures will be used by you to calculate the sales per square foot of floor space in the store. This is done by dividing the sales for a given period in a department by the number of square feet of floor space in the department. The knowledge of sales per square feet will help you determine the amount of space needed for a product. If sunglasses represent 15 percent of the sales in your accessory shop, then you know what space allocation it needs. Knowing sales results will help you determine whether your budget needs adjusting up or down. Sales results will help you allocate amounts of money that should be used to improve the sales potential of a department and where to spend the money for better presentation. Being aware of sales results helps you support management decisions. With this knowledge you become aware of and support sales trends. □

8

Signage

S igns are silent sales associates. Signs are often responsible for the first contact customers have with a store, a department within the store, and the merchandise within the department. (Figures 8-1 and 8-2) Good signs identify departments, describe the merchandise and its price, tell customers about special sales events, signal customers about advertised merchandise, and identify the theme of special window and interior displays. Other signs direct customers to department locations, describe store hours, inform customers about non-selling locations such as the credit department, store office, and restrooms and warn customers about wet floors and inoperable elevators and doors.

Merchandise signs describe the merchandise and its price. Keep them brief and concise. Choose copy that accurately describes the merchandise. Keep the copy short enough to hold the customers' attention. Customers will not stand for long periods of time reading several paragraphs about the merchandise. Keep the pricing on the signs as simple as possible. Complicated pricing tends to confuse customers. Be careful not to be vague when composing a sign. Phrases such as "Spring Arrivals," "New Merchandise," and "New Fall Looks" are somewhat redundant since the customers assume that all the merchandise is timely, current, and fresh. All signs should be in sign holders. A sloppy effect is created by taping signs to fixtures.

The merchandising staff requests most of the signs that are produced by

8-1 Klaus Berger, Calgary, Alberta

8-2 Fendi, Troy MI

8-3 Cin-tec Plastics, Cincinnati OH

the visual merchandising department. The merchandising staff knows when new merchandise will be available and when it will be displayed; therefore, it knowns when new signs are needed for the merchandise. The staff must provide you with enough information about the merchandise and the cost of the merchandise to permit you to make the necessary signs. Department managers will have some idea about the quantities of the sign that are needed. It is your responsibility to work with the merchandising staff to be sure you understand the timing of the merchandise displays and have the correct copy and prices for the signs.

Merchandising associates tend to want too many signs and signs that are too large for the merchandise. A sign should not be so big that it upstages the merchandise. A proliferation of signs for a class of merchandise will add clutter to the display and detract from the merchandise. No customer wants to read a dozen repetitious signs. Too many unnecessary signs create a sense of monotony that shoppers might associate with the store's merchandise. Since the merchandise is presented in an orderly manner by its class, it is imperative that your signs identify the class in an orderly manner.

Choose cardboard stock and type faces for signs very carefully. Signs should be easy to read and aesthetically pleasing. White is the accepted color for general merchandise signs. Signs printed on various colors of card stock create a disorderly appearance. Special card colors can be used very effectively for merchandise sales and clearances. Keep in mind that colored inks and cardboards used for both clearance and general merchandise tend to confuse the customers.

Select sign type faces for readability and legibility. Readability refers to the arrangement of the type, which affects the ease by which a customer can read a sign. Legibility refers to the design of the type, which affects the speed with which a customer can read a sign. In addition, the type style should reflect as nearly as possible your store's image, the price points of the merchandise, the quality of the merchandise, and the fashion image your store wants to project. There are many possibilities — the type style might be a modification of the store's logo or the type design might reflect the style used in the store's advertising. Try to pick a style that projects a clear, strong statement. If you need help with type selection, check with your type suppliers as they have many studies available that can help you make your choice.

Maintenance of general merchandise signs is a must. Smudged, dirty signs indicate poor housekeeping. They probably indicate to your customers that the merchandise is not clean and fresh. It is important that the general merchandise signs are current. Price points change and if the signs do not reflect these changes, the store might be forced to sell the goods at the prices listed on the signs. Be aware that sales associates sometimes mutilate signs when they make price changes with pencils or

123

when they glue a new price over an old one. Also, it stretches the store's credibility when customers read signs that say "Spring Colors" during the summertime. Check all signs on a daily basis to make sure they are current. Remove signs and their holders immediately after a sale or an event.

If your store is small, all general merchandise signs within a class of merchandise should be the same size. Signs used to price merchandise stored on shelves or on the same fixture should be consistent, that is, they should be the same size, same color, and printed with the same type face. To be most effective, signs must have constant locations. For example, if some signs are located on the shelf faces, then all the signs must be located there. Customers develop habits of looking to the same locations for signs. There is no good reason to distract customers who are trying to make choices from a wide array of goods by having them to look for price signs. Signs that describe a group of merchandise should be larger than price signs and can be appropriately displayed on top of the rows of shelving or fixtures.

As you know, a department store is a group of small stores under a central management. The department store is developed to house wide varieties of merchandise and departments. In contrast, a small store is limited in space and thus limited in the amount of merchandise it can display. For example, a small women's apparel shop might have only a collection of moderately priced sportswear representing a specific fashion and in size be equal to one department of a department store. Whether you work in a small shop or a department store with its many stores, the rules for preparing and presenting signs remain the same.

Your signs should be consistent. If, for example, you are planning signs for an apparel shop or an apparel department, signs that describe the merchandise will be needed for the tops of the apparel racks. If you choose a 7" x 11" sign for the top of one rack, you should choose the same size for all the racks. In a china shop or department, all the merchandise signs are placed on counters, cubes, or tables. Whatever size sign you choose for these fixtures, be sure to choose the same size for all china merchandise descriptions. Place larger signs that identify the overall merchandise groups in front of the departments. These signs could be placed on the floor. Be careful to use as many signs as needed but not so many that they clutter the department. A word about sign holders — since these signs will be changed frequently because of price changes, new merchandise arrivals, and special sales, well-designed, durable sign holders that permit quick and efficient location changes are a good investment. (Figure 8-3)

Sign copy should include a significant headline, merchandise description, and price. An example follows:

Down Jackets . . . . Headline
Warm Nylon Fleece . . . . Description (Body Copy)
$000.00 . . . . Price

Vary the type size used on the signs. The headline for a 7" x 11" landscape or horizontal sign might be 100 points. The merchandise description (body copy) should be smaller, perhaps 40 points. The price would generally be no larger than the headline but larger than the merchandise description. For example, it might be 80 points. There are no hard and fast rules to follow about varying type sizes and layout designs, except that they should be readable and aesthetically pleasing.

Sign requisitions are used by the merchandise staff to order signs from the visual merchandising department. Large department stores use thousands of requisitions, which are designed to be very specific. Information needed on the requisitions include: sign size and quantity; quantities for specific stores; date due; ordering department; department location; advertising tie-in; ad date; special event; event date; buyer ordering sign; and date requisition received by the display department. In the space for copy instructions, the buyer must insert the headline, merchandise description, and price. This is necessary for the sign maker to compose the layout and print the sign.

Every store has its own sign needs and the requisitions must be tailored to the particular company. Small stores often use simple mimeographed forms as sign requisitions, while others use universal forms supplied by fixture supply houses. Depending on the size of the company, it takes from two to ten days to process and make signs. Buyers should provide enough lead time when ordering signs to assure delivery of the signs when they are needed. Copy composition is very important. All stores have a specific style to describe merchandise, sales and events. Large department stores employ copy writers to compose the appropriate copy.

Signs are needed to describe groups of merchandise in a department that are larger than general merchandise description signs. These large signs are used to signal customers that all the merchandise in the department is on sale or the merchandise is featured in a special manner. A department will need less of these signs than the specific merchandise signs. These signs might be on the order of 11" x 14" or 14" x 22" in size and be mounted in a vertical position. Rather than being on a fixture, they will stand on the floor in front of a department. These signs should be out of the way of customer traffic and be clear of the department aisles so they do not barricade customers from entering the department. Larger type styles than are used for the specific merchandise signs are necessary, but generally the large signs will have the same layout designs as the specific merchandise signs.

Perimeter merchandise signs describe the merchandise housed in wall cabanas or on shelving. Perimeter sign card holders can be fastened to the wall, hung from light cornices, or mounted on a dress rod in a cabana. These signs generally range up to 7" x 11" in size. Great care should be taken with the placement of these signs. Avoid cluttered arrangements because the back wall of a department is conspicuous. Mount the signs to conform with the architectural lines of the walls. The aesthetic lines of the architecture will dictate the sign positions. Do not mount the signs too high, because this makes reading of the signs difficult and takes the customers eyes up and away from the merchandise. Clean perimeter merchandise presentation and sign placement helps the customers see the merchandise in an orderly manner.

Shop signs are used to identify the various departments in the store such as housewares, sportswear, and shoes. These signs must be uniform in letter sizes, letter styles, letter colors, and background colors. The use of different letter sizes, styles, and colors for each shop produces a spotty, disorganized appearance. The architectural design of the store will dictate the placement of these signs. They should be placed high enough so that the customers can read them from a distance. Generally speaking, these signs should be located on the centers of the department back walls.

Shop identification signs are not printed or screened on sign presses. They are made by applying letters directly to the wall or by mounting the letters on plexiglas or other rigid materials and applying the sign to the back wall. Display suppliers sell these individual letters, available in many different styles and colors and fabricated from many different materials. Custom letters can be made for special designs. These signs must be in keeping with the style and color of the store's decor.

Sub-department signs are used to identify sub-categories of merchandise within a department, such as special designer clothes or merchandise that is on sale. These signs are small and they are positioned in cabanas, on light cornices, and on perimeter fixtures. The sign mountings should be flexible, since they will be moved around as the location of the merchandise is changed from time to time. The sub-department signs are usually screened on plexiglas to give them a permanent appearance. Again, the consistent use of the same letter styles, sizes, and color in the signs gives them a uniform appearance, permitting customers to concentrate on the merchandise instead of the signs. Letter sizes up to 6" or 8" should be chosen for department and shop names. Store associates believe that larger letters and signs will attract more customers. However, customers are able to identify most merchandise when they are standing in front of a department. They know what shop it is. A cleaner design statement is effected if the shop signs are smaller. The letter size also depends on the size of the shop, the ceiling height, and the size of the shop's back wall. Try to choose the smallest readable letters. Letter sizes up to 2" can be used for column or back wall mounted signs.

General information signs that include store hours, store special events, all-over sales events, and departmental sales events are placed on the floor at each entrance to the store. These poster signs are best printed on 22" x 28" card stock and they are mounted vertically. They can be colorful and decorative. Combined type styles and illustrations can be used effectively; however, information such as store hours should be readable at a glance. Colored card stock and inks can be used to match the colors of the seasons or to match the colors associated with the sales event. A word of warning, though — if you use too many signs at each entrance, they will lose their impact since customers will not take enough time to read all of them. You should not use more than two general information signs at each entrance.

An on-hand stock of printed 11" x 14" vertical signs for emergencies are needed. They cover such sujects as: "Wet Floors," "Washroom Out Of Order," "Do Not Use This Door," and "Elevator Out Of Order."

Sign holders are made from many different materials and they are available from many different suppliers. Select sign holders for their design simplicity, flexibility, and ease of maintenance. The use of too many sign holders of varying finishes and designs will create a disorderly look. Sign holders get dirty and covered with fingerprints, so choose holders that are easy to wash and not subject to corrosion. If your sign holder choice is bright chrome, make sure that all the holders have a bright chrome finish. Even though bright chrome is your first choice, you might have occasions to use plexiglas holders. By all means, buy them. However, do not buy them in the same quantities as the bright chrome finished holders. Let your preferred choice, the bright chrome, dominate your sign holder stock by at least 80 percent. All the sign holders should be the same design.

Sign holders accept 5½" x 7", 7" x 11", 11" x 14", 14" x 22", and 22" x 28" cards. (Figure 8-4) These sizes are universal. The size is determined by the standard card stock 22" x 28"; all sizes are an equal division of this size. The holders are available with clamps and stems for attachment to apparel racks and apparel bars, stems and pedestals for placement on counter tops, pedestals and bases for floor locations, and some are designed to be mounted on walls. Practically any variations necessary to provide signs for a store are available from fixture supply houses.

In small stores, most signs can be printed in the display department with a 14" x 22" sign machine. Also, signs can be made by using adhesive-backed or stick-pin type letters. Signs that require hand lettering can be made by you or sent out to calligraphers' studios. Limit the use of hand-lettered signs to special window displays. General merchandise signs should always be printed on the sign machine. (Figures 8-5 and 8-6) Large department stores have a separate sign departments staffed by managers, copy writers, sign makers, calligraphers, and clerks. Because of this specialization, uniform signs are produced on a timely basis. This helps the over all appearance of the stores.

Large sign departments use silk screens and sophisticated sign machines to print signs. (Figure 8-7) Manufacturers of printing equipment can help you decide what printing machinery is appropriate for your store, and can also provide you with type. Many letter styles are available and they are

8-4 Cin-tec Plastics, Cincinnati OH

8-5 Foto Star, City of Industry CA

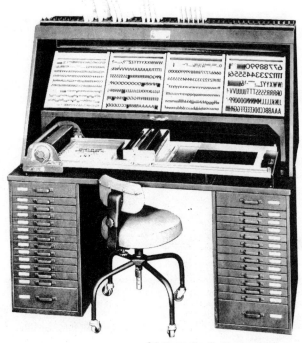

8-6 Morgan Sign Machine Co., Chicago IL

8-7 Cugher, Minneapolis MN

8-8　Pot Pourri, Toronto, Ontario

BRIGHT IDEAS BY INGRI

8-9　Lechmere, Woburn MA

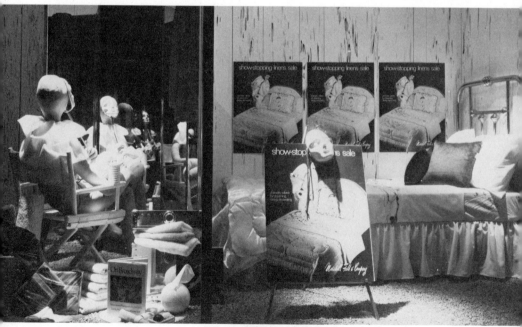

8-10　Marshall Field's, Calumet City IL

sold in fonts, which are complete assortments of all the letters and characters of one size and style of type. Choose fonts of varying sizes, limiting type face design to one.

Character counting is the most accurate method for determining the space needed for printing copy on a sign. This consists of counting all the characters and spaces in sign copy. Then you divide the number of characters per inch of the type style and size you have selected for the sign into the number of characters in the copy. This results in the number of inches you will need for printing. Type manufacturers can supply charts that list the number of characters per inch of all sizes and the most common type face.

Windows and special in-store displays require special signs. (Figures 8-8, 8-9, 8-10, and 8-11) The design, color, style, materials, and the placement of the materials must be related to the design principles of your display. Letters that are hand-painted, silk screened, or made from natural materials (anything from bricks to tree branches) can be used in windows and displays. Special lighting for signs, back-lighted letters, light from spot sources, all-over lighting or light from neon can be effectively used, provided it is in keeping with the composition style, and design of your window or in-store display. Copy for the display or window signs should be brief, but it can be humorous, descriptive, or theme related. The mood of a display can be established by one short line of copy or one word. Sometimes letters can be used as graphic elements in a display. Words can be repeated, creating a graphics effect. If physically large enough, they can be part of the backdrop for a display or cover the entire wall as a display backdrop. The merchandise can be arranged to spell out words.

Store directories must be located at prominent aisles, and by the elevators and escalators. The directories help customers locate merchandise, store departments, and non-selling areas. Some stores use only copy to describe department locations, while others use drawings of the store floor plans for this. Directories are designed to hang on a wall or be floor mounted. They can be internally or externally lighted.

Sign toppers are signs that are cut at the bottom to slide over the top of another sign in a sign holder. These are add-on type signs that are used to notify customers of sales or special merchandise events. They must be attention-getting; therefore, they should be printed in a conspicuous color. Over-exposure of the toppers will lessen the impact of each sale. The toppers must only be used to identify significant sales. Customers lose confidence if you over-dramatize a sale or if you try to make a lesser sale more important than it is. These toppers can be used and removed, not disturbing the general merchandise sign.

Banners are an effective way of making signs for some retailers. Generally, these banners are vertical in shape and are suspended from the store's ceiling. They are made of fabric, vinyl, or any other suitable

131

8-11   Z.C.M.I., Salt Lake City UT

8-12   Howard Int'l. Corp., New York NY

materials. Banners should carry messages only about the most significant special events, merchandise events or establish a seasonal theme. Banners attract the most attention when they are designed like a graphic. The most efficient use of banners is to hang them in groups so that their message is repeated many times. Good locations for banners are on each column along main aisles or clustered together in a department. Banners must be designed and hung to complement the store's dominant architectural lines. You can make an architectural design statement with them. At Christmastime, banners can be used to better distribute your Christmas theme. A sales message in red or green with a screened wreath will project the Christmas idea and signal a special message to the customers. Some stores make it a point to use banners as part of their Christmas store trim.

The name of the store must appear on the exterior of the building. Store identification signs can be either free standing or wall-mounted, and can be made from a wide range of materials. The style of the letters in the sign should reflect the store's image and quality of merchandise it sells. The store logo can be incorporated into the sign to enhance identification. The letters can be internally-lighted, back-lighted, or illuminated with spotlights. But do not be so anxious to make the sign visible that it overpowers the store architecture. Signs that are too gaudy can have a negative effect on customers. Also, remember that shopping malls and villages have ordinances that specify the materials, size, and locations for signs.

Vendor fixtures, signs, and posters are supplied to your store to house the vendor's merchandise. (Figure 8-12) These fixtures are bought by the vendor or manufactured by a fixture company to the vendor's specifications. They usually have their company name prominently displayed on top of the fixture. A word about these fixtures supplied by vendors: because they have their company names or trademarks (logos) on them and because each vendor uses a different type, style and color to print his logo, the fixtures produce a cluttered look when they are combined with your signs. Fixtures and signs with prominent logos should rarely be used. You want to emphasize your store's name and not your vendor's. If you wish to feature a vendor's name, you should work with the vendor and have him supply his logo in a form that is consistent with the design of your store and your sign policy. □

9

Store
Planning

S tore planning is needed for new stores, for department relocation, for fixture replacement, for remodelling, and for the placement of merchandise on the selling floor. Store planners organize all the store's space with the guidance of the merchandising staff.

The new store is planned by the in-house staff or by a consulting architectural firm. Architectural and design firms specialize in store planning. The planning and installation can be totally handled by outside firms, or they might do only part of it, leaving some of the task to the store's construction and design team. The store might want to plan and buy fixtures from its own sources, leaving the space planning to a consulting firm.

When a store is planned, the space must reflect the store's fashion image, merchandise program, and attitude. (Figure 9-1) The size and location of each department must reflect the store's merchandising plan and goals. The merchandising management group will analyze the store's market and scale each department's size to represent the percent of that department's business to the total store business. The location of each department will be determined by its appropriate proximity to traffic areas that reflect its volume potential. High volume departments that represent the store's greatest percent of business and the store's highest volume will be located close to the high traffic entrances and next to high traffic aisles and escalators on the main floor. Low volume and low profit departments will be placed on other floors in areas of less traffic. (Figure 9-2) The depart-

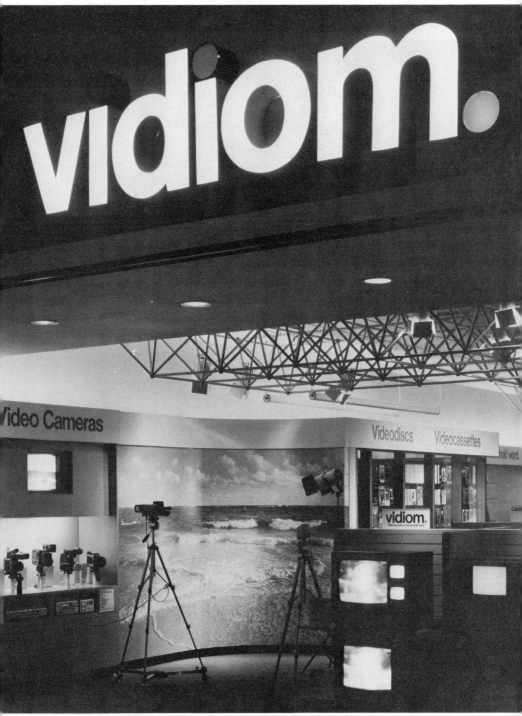

9-1 Vidiom, Richmond CA

9-2 Woodward & Lothrop, White Marsh MD

9-3 Woodward & Lothrop, White Marsh MD

ments must be grouped so that related businesses are together, such as women's apparel next to cosmetics and accessories, or television sets next to major applicances. Good proximities help the customer locate merchandise categories and allow the store to staff sales associates in departments that can establish inter-selling.

Stock and operating space must be allocated in ratios between selling space and non-selling space. The operating management will help plan adequate space for supportive services. The merchandising management will plan properly sized stock areas that reflect the need for merchandise handling, preparation and merchandise storage. The merchandising management will plan the correct size of space for customer services.

A budget for the project is determined by management. Amounts of money will be set aside for construction, labor, lighting, signs, fixtures, carpets and flooring, furniture, wall covering, hardware, consulting costs and all the money it takes to complete the project. These costs are capital expenditures. They are costs that are amortized over a period of time and are costs that are benefited with certain tax credits. Money for such projects is borrowed, creating an interest charge, another cost factor. It is important that new store planning is good and thorough and that it is cost effective.

A sales-per-square-foot analysis should be made to determine the size for each department. The anticipated sales volume, divided by the anticipated sales-per-square-foot, will give you an idea of the department space needed. Not all departments can produce maximum dollars per square foot. The furniture department is a good example of a large department which produces less dollar volume for its size. Some departments need a larger ratio of space to do business because of the merchandise size. Departments that produce low profitability because of low markup cannot command lots of space even though the sales volume is high. Stores that specialize in these low profit categories will need more space for impacting and housing that merchandise. A higher budget is allocated to buy better fixtures and to better furnish departments that represent the store's specialty, strength or glamour. (Figure 9-3) If women's apparel represents thirty percent of the store's business, then thirty percent of the budget and effort should be given that category. If you have an expensive apparel shop within the store's apparel department, more money and time will be spent on it than on the general apparel area.

Segregated rooms that create shops are being dropped from store planning because of their cost. Better merchandise is being located within classification. For example, designer sportswear is integrated into the sportswear department. This merchandise identified by class makes shopping easier for the customer and reduces the cost of special sales help. More money can be spent on a better look for the total sportswear department. In branch stores, customers feel a little conspicuous in a segregated shop.

9-4 Van Leunen's, Fairfield OH

9-5 Van Leunen's, Fairfield OH

Special zones can be created to highlight better merchandise or designer merchandise within a parent department. The quality of light fixtures and special signs can emphasize the higher price points. The adjacency of the merchandise of higher price points next to merchandise of popular price points may stimulate the customer to "trade up." Within the sportswear category one might separate moderate, better, and updated sportswear. A department can be handsomely designed to give identity to these classifications and thus allow the customer to see all sportswear as a whole.

The quantity of merchandise needed to produce the sales volume will determine the number of fixtures needed for each department. A variety of fixtures are needed in each department to house each class. Some fixtures will be needed to house mass stock, and others to highlight groups, fashion presentation, price variation, and advertised merchandise. (Figures 9-4 and 9-5) Other fixtures within the department will be needed to house classes of merchandise that provide the department with an image.

For an apparel department, modules will be needed for the perimeter of the department. Hanging rods, face-out bars and shelves should be planned for the back wall. (Figure 9-6) Rods are needed to hang large quantities of stock. Face-out bars are needed to break up this configuration and to highlight the stock for fashion interest. Shelves are needed to place folded merchandise. This hardware mix further breaks up the monotony of a totally rodded cabana wall. The modules should be designed with adequate mirrors for the customers. The design should provide supportive color families and proper lighting to create the mood that best represents the stock's identity. The back wall should have special signs to identify the merchandise category, as well as large signs to identify the departments. Back walls should be designed in modules wide enough to accommodate groups, but not too wide to overpower a class group of merchandise. Smaller group divisions of merchandise eliminate monotony.

Fitting rooms must be located conveniently for the customer, close to the selling floor. Privacy, adequate lighting, and comfort are some of the design requirements. Colors and lighting for the fitting rooms should be chosen with care to flatter the customer and merchandise. Theft prevention should be a design consideration when designing the department and fitting rooms. Barriers or partitions that obstruct visibility should be avoided. Shrinkage occurs when shoplifters have privacy.

Large circular or straight racks are needed to hang the bulk stock. These fixtures must be considered for flexibility, sturdiness, and good design. The large fixtures should be arranged in the back zone of the department in front of the back wall. Smaller four-arm fixtures should be up front, and T-stands should be placed at the very front aisle line. Fashion and feature merchandise should be hung on these fixtures. T-stands are especially needed to highlight a few pieces for an advertisement or to impact a fashion look. All fixtures should be of the same finish and design. 139

9-6 Sak's, Manhattan NY

9-7 Nordstrom, Seattle WA

140

Cubes and mannequins are needed for the front of the department. The cubes can be grouped as platforms for groups of mannequins or to serve as a support on which draped or folded merchandise is presented. A group of at least four mannequins is needed up front to tell fashion stories and to present fashion merchandise. (Figure 9-7) Several mannequins provide the opportunity for you to impact the merchandise better, because several items of similar merchandise together creates a stronger impression than one.

Invest in good mannequins and buy from companies that are known for fashion leadership. Studies show that the customer receives more fashion information from seeing merchandise on mannequins than she does from an advertisement, a fashion show, or a fashion magazine. This provides you with a great opportunity to do suggestive selling and to emphasize your fashion image.

Interesting display tables can be combined with display cubes to create an interesting up-front look. Large plexi or glass display cubicles can be grouped together to house folded merchandise.

It is important to count the units of merchandise to be housed in the department so you can plan adequate back wall space, circle racks, four-arm fixtures, T-stands, fixtures for folded stock, display tables, and display cubes. Some racks can house 120 pieces of apparel, others 12 pieces. Cabanas can house 50 to 75 pieces per module, depending on their size. Heavy outer apparel demands more space per fixture because of their bulk. All merchants want to get as much stock on the floor as possible. Some editing must be done to create a good balance of goods on the floor and to eliminate the look of over-crowding.

A location must be decided on for the cash wrap or point of sale (p-o-s). The p-o-s must be placed in a convenient visible location.

Adequate aisle space must be considered. A simple rectangular grid configuration should be used for fixture placement. It is important to have clean sight lines from the front of the department to the back and from side to side. Short fixtures should be up front; tall ones in back so as not to obstruct the customer's view. This arrangment eliminates a cluttered look. The grid plan allows you to have enormous amounts of stock on the floor from time to time without producing a crowded look. The plan enables you to establish an orderly look on the selling floor.

Many stores are adopting a customer self selection system. With spiralling operating costs, management has decided to make many selling departments self service. This system allows a store to operate a department with fewer selling associates. The merchandise must be presented with a high profile, since it has to sell itself. Fixtures chosen must make the merchandise look irresistible and the merchandise must be easily accessible. Glass show cases that are not self service are used only for merchandise that is priced high and that is a shrinkage risk. In stores that are self service, it is

9-8 Crowley, Milner & Co., Warren MI

9-9 J. L. Hudson, Kalamazoo MI

important to present merchandise by class and not lifestyle. The customer will find merchandise easier if presented by class.

Old types of selling bases and cases are being replaced with simple flexible cubes. (Figures 9-8 and 9-9) These cubes are being used in the china department, housewares department, foods department, linens department, and wherever the cubes adapt to the merchandise presentation and ease of selling the merchandise. The cubes generally look best clustered in groups of three or four, and their sizes should vary as well as their height. This variation helps break a monotonous look of all goods seen at the same level. It also helps to show merchandise within a classification. The size of the cubes should be determined by the number of multiple merchandise classes within the major classification. The number of cubes for a shoe department will be determined by how many shoes are shown in the department. The number of groups of cubes will be determined by classification. Evening shoes, career shoes, casual shoes, athletic shoes, sport shoes, and dress shoes are but a few classifications to be grouped in clusters on cubes. Further classification breakdown within a class is necessary. Within the sport shoes group cluster, it would be wise to group espadrilles on an additional cube cluster. The cubes should relate to the dominant color and textural theme of the selling department. The best color family to use is the neutrals, and the texture should not be strong to interfere with the merchandise impact. The cubes should be simple in design with surfaces that are easily maintained.

The cubes should be arranged in clusters on a grid plan. Sight lines must be established from the front to the back of the department, allowing wide aisles for the customers. Good aisles and sight lines must also be established laterally across the department.

The perimeter of self service departments must be fixtured with wall hung units that are flexible and allow the merchandise to be shown clearly and within class. The merchandise must be very accessible to the customer. The signs must relate in color and style to the selling department, and must be easily read, simple and to the point.

Fixtures should be chosen for their ability to adapt to the changes in season. Classes of merchandise and their quantities will change from season to season. In women's apparel, lengths change as well as fabrication. Winter merchandise is bulky. A dress rack may hold one-fourth less fall merchandise because of its bulk. Swimwear and coats are classes that are not in stock at certain times of the year. Appropriate flexible fixtures that convert from dresses to coats must be selected.

Floor plans and elevation plans must be drawn to help in planning stages. These plans are generally drawn to 1:16 scale. The floor plans show every detail of the floor. They show the size of the departments and their locations, where the columns are, changes in the floor grade, the locations of stairways, and where fixtures are to be placed. The drawings allow the

143

9-10 Shillito's, Cincinnati OH

designer to plan and see how to establish traffic aisles and traffic patterns and where and how carpet is laid. These floor plans allow the merchandising associates to determine the size of the department and modify its size to the ratio of merchandise he plans to present or stock. After each new store opening, it often happens that one or two departments were designed too large or too small either for the projected business or for the quantities of merchandise that it is expected to hold. The popularity of merchandise can change from year to year, and it may be found that the store is selling more or less of a merchandise class.

The elevation drawings will show all the perimeter walls of the selling department. These drawings will help you plan for perimeter fixtures, perimeter lighting, and for proper signing. The drawings are used as a guide for color selection and wallpaper selection. These drawings are used as a guide to help you plan the height of the fixtures on the floor, as well as those on the perimeter walls.

Small enclosed shops in department stores are being eliminated wherever it is feasible. Many of these shops do not generate enough sales volume to warrant staffing with sales associates. The customer does not seem to take time to walk through these small shops. Shrinkage is another problem.

Great care should be taken when planning the store or any of the store's departments to make them as visually interesting as possible. Customers can shop at any number of department stores around the country and be faced with virtually the same merchandise offerings in each. Display areas should be given adequate up front space so that new arrivals, advertised merchandise, and merchandise image can be expressed. (Figure 9-10) These display areas should be uniquely lighted to segregate and highlight the merchandise, making it look irresistible. Choose fixtures that express quality and style. Whether they are in the form of cubes and mannequins for apparel, or fixtures that house glassware or a table setting, they should be selected for flexibility and for their ability to clearly display the merchandise. (Figure 9-11)

Choose fixtures that relate to the merchandise mix. Trendy, updated merchandise should be housed on fixtures that relate to that style; other merchandise categories will require more sedate looking fixtures. In the search for varied, interesting fixtures, you might find at market that only fifty percent of them relate to the look you want. It is important to have some custom made fixtures, and any number of fixture manufacturers can provide this service. If you have an in-store carpenter shop, some fixture making and modification can be done there.

Retailers want to increase their sales per square foot. It is up to you to maximize each inch of the store, making it sales productive. The fixtures must be designed and positioned on the selling floor in a manner that will generate the greatest sales. After the department has been planned and

9-11 O. C. Tanner Co., Salt Lake City UT

created, it is important to watch it carefully, replacing old fixtures with new ones to reflect changing merchandise strategies. A close monitor of the sales will help you decide to enlarge or reduce the department size or to rearrange the fixtures and classes of merchandise to increase sales.

A budget should be established for replacement fixtures and to cover the costs of modifying selling departments. So often after the department has been installed, management neglects it. It begins to look shabby, the fixtures no longer properly house new kinds of merchandise and sales are lost as a result. A new fixture cost is so minor compared to the amount of goods sold from it daily. It is not uncommon to have a dress rack produce sales in one day that are double the cost of the rack. With fewer sales associates to sell the merchandise, it is wise to spend money on the fixtures that sell the merchandise.

Special shops for Christmas merchandise and shops that are developed to sell seasonal goods are sales generators if planned well. These shops are short lived. Proper fixtures must be budgeted for them. These shops are often made adjuncts or replace parts of departments that for one reason or another produce less sales at that time. The additional new shop might increase interest and boost sales of the parent department. These shops must be dramatized and impacted sufficiently to look separate from the existing department. A change in the light level will help you achieve this. Careful color planning and proper signing will also help you give the shop identity and impact it. These shops should be located in traffic areas that relate to the kind of volume that is planned. Retailers often rehabilitate fixtures for special shops. If proper budgets have not been planned to buy fixtures or to furnish special shops, then this is obvious by their look and as a result the sales are never maximized. Christmas trim-the-tree shops, Christmas card shops, and Christmas gift and outpost shops are a few that are temporary and need special design consideration.

New fixtures are continually being designed for new products and shopping habits. As lifestyles are forever changing and as technology advances create new products, the retailer must constantly look for new fixtures. From cosmetic manufacturers to small appliance manufacturers, they are all trying to develop appropriate fixtures to house their products. Many of these fixtures reflect current decorative trends and can be used as part of your store planning. Fixture manufacturers are forever creating items that are made from exciting new materials, such as sleek glass, plexi, and chrome.

Retailers often develop specific store looks, creating new decorative trends. Within a short period of time, these decorative looks and trends are copied by retailers across the country. As a designer, you must select and modify the looks that best fit your store's merchandising philosophy. One cannot be too esoteric in choice of the decor, because the customer will not relate to it and one would have a difficult time finding the decorative   147 material to do the job. The fixtures must be selected so they relate in design, color, and texture to the wall colors, wallpaper, and decorative furnishings of the department.

The installation of a new department will require the teamwork of a large staff. Carpenters, rug layers, painters, and electricians supervised by the architectural group and store planners will build and shape the space. The visual merchandising group and store planners place and install the display and merchandise fixtures. The merchandise team will place the merchandise on the floor on the fixtures. The fashion and VM team will refine the merchandise placement so that it is visually appealing. The VM and fashion groups will display the merchandise in the frontal display area, as well as placing all the merchandise in the departments in proper order. The timing for this team effort must be carefully worked out so that everything is scheduled in the right order.

Excellent advanced planning must be done so that all the materials needed for the department's construction, fixturing, and furnishing are purchased and delivered for the completion deadline. The merchandise must be bought and delivered to coincide with this date. The energies of all the store's personnel are needed to develop and complete a new department or store. Accountants and financial officers will establish budgets for the merchandise, construction, fixtures and furnishings. Buyers will buy merchandise and planners will buy fixtures. Hundreds of details from plumbing to carpeting, personnel to security, must be worked out.

The ease of maintenance is a consideration when designing or selecting a fixture or product for the store's interior. Few stores have in-store housecleaning services. They prefer using janitorial services. Contracts with janitorial services often do not include detail cleaning. It is therefore important to choose rug fabrics that will produce long life and are easy to clean. Fixtures, furniture, drapery materials, and upholstery materials must be chosen for their ability to repel soil and for cleaning ease. Neutral color families or colors in the middle gray scale show dirt and soil less than others. Fabrics and rugs with patterns disguise soil. If simple small patterns fit the decorative plan, then choose fabrics that suggest pattern by their weave and color variation and mix, such as tweed.

Broadloom carpet should be of heavy-weight wool for long wear. Wool is the king fiber for both wear and cleaning. Often area rugs are placed over resilient flooring, which helps define the floor space and allows the designer to use the floor as a design. Slate, marble, vinyl, wood, cobblestones, and brick are resilient flooring materials that will be long lasting. The finish of these materials should be made relatively nonporous to eliminate dirt retention. Their colors and texture must relate to the dominant decor theme of the selling space.

All the materials must be chosen for their ability to resist fire and be noncombustible. All materials cannot meet these guidelines, but it is wise to build that factor into the planning.

Traffic aisles are created by laying carpet in rectangular or geometric patterns large enough to define the selling space or department and by planning perimeter aisles made of resilient flooring materials. Change the light levels from department to department and aisle to aisle to further establish a visual difference. Proper signs will help identify the departments.

If the store has several levels, it is important to develop interesting departments on the additional levels to generate traffic. Departments that are often relegated to the back of the an upper floor should receive an updated colorful look to help generate traffic, but not a color that overpowers the merchandise.

Escalators, stairs, and elevators should be grouped and positioned to move shoppers easily and quickly from floor to floor. Escalators generate centers of traffic, so departments that produce high sales should be grouped close to the escalators, stairs, or elevators. The escalators and stairs must be planned so that they do not take up valuable selling space. On the other hand, they must not be remotely located, making them obscure or difficult to reach.

Departments should be planned with perimeter aisles wide enough to move traffic. Aisles should be developed in each department, smaller in width than perimeter aisles but wide enough to disperse traffic into and through the department. The proper grid placement of fixtures will establish the inner department aisles. The inner department aisles should be planned to provide good sight lines from the front to the rear of the department and from side to side. The fixtures should be grouped so that they relate in size to the customer's scope. Large blocks and groups of fixtures and merchandise can overwhelm the customers, confusing their ability to make a selection.

Some stores over-light and over-scale home furnishings departments. A furniture or table linens department should be designed to re-create a residential look and ambient feeling. In this atmosphere, the customer will have an easier time selecting merchandise and determining how it relates to her own interior. The image, use, price, texture and style of the merchandise should be strongly emphasized in the design of the department. A glass department should look like glass, with reflective materials that are light in color and shiny. Lots of light produced by a variety of fixtures to produce multiple light levels will further enhance the merchandise and dramatize the look of the department. If you choose a single theme for a department, everything you choose for developing its design should relate to and reflect that theme.

Stores that are planned with an open look and have no walls separating merchandise categories must use an all-over design and color theme that sets the tone of each of the merchandise groups and departments. Slight color changes should be created for department identity. Fixtures must change their look from department to department in a subtle way. One must keep an overall look in mind. If very dramatic design and color changes are used, a jarring visual effect will be created.

New designs for stores are forever being created. In the planning stages, it is wise to travel to other stores in cities across the country to see how effective their plans have been. Borrow and distill the best designs for your plans. On these trips, you will see the work of the other planners and consulting firms. After viewing their work, it will help you decide what firms can be hired to consult with you and the management on your store planning. Seeing the best and the worst might save you great amounts of money by enabling you do develop the best possible looks and avoiding those that would be a disaster.

Adequate amounts of money should be spent to create the interiors that you have planned. Profits will be realized by generating sales, not cost cutting. Appropriate amounts of money must be spent to increase sales.

A planner must, after having planned major fixturing, plan secondary fixturing. Tie racks for counter tops, leg forms for the hosiery department, risers for shoes in the shoe department, and sign holders are but a few fixtures that fit that category. The china department should be supplied with plate holders. The blouse and scarf department must be supplied with countertop draping stands. Plexi-boxes must be considered for countertop merchandise organizers. Bicycle stands and lawn mower stands must be bought for the toy and appliance departments. All of the secondary fixtures must be made of the same materials, be finished in the same colors, and be designed in the same style as the major fixtures.

Some sign holders mount on a wall, but most of the holders needed will be the floor type. The sign sizes are determined by card sizes available from paper suppliers. The basic size is 22" x 28", from which other sizes can be cut: 14" x 22", 11" x 14", 7" x 11", and 5½" x 7". The number of card holders is determined by the fixtures selected. The 22" x 28" sign holders are used at entry ways or in high traffic areas to announce events, store hours, institutional information, and major sales. Fewer of these sign holders will be needed than the 11" x 14" and 5½" x 7" signs, which are used on counter tops to describe the merchandise and its price. The 7" x 11" card is the favorite size for most retailers because the information printed with average size type is easily read and most copy fits this size card. Too many signs can be annoying to a customer. They create a cluttered look, often overpowering the merchandise and supplying more information than the customer wants to read.

The back walls or perimeter walls of a department must be considered for merchandise presentation. The appropriate hardware must be selected to best show this merchandise. Make the decision to use peg board and the right type of hooks, and determine whether a wall should be shelved for folded merchandise or to hold boxed merchandise. The type of shelving, glass or wood, is an important factor. Some apparel walls will be rodded or bars mounted for waterfall arms and the appropriate mounting hardware must be chosen. There are hardware companies that supply retailers with components that are intended to augment fixturing, such as shelf brackets, apparel hangers, rods, and key striping.

Non-selling and operating space planning is essential. Restaurants, kitchens, washrooms, alteration departments, personnel departments, stock rooms, receiving areas, offices, credit departments, customer service, and the display department all require space. They all have special task areas and equipment needed. Develop plans with the management of each area, making sure that each detail is carefully worked out. Space allocation must be provided for each operation. Restaurants, some key offices, the credit department, personnel department, and customer service department are areas where customers will be. The decor should be functional but pleasant for the customers. Refined decorative materials should be chosen to attractively decorate these high profile non-selling areas.

Work areas must be painted with pleasing colors to encourage work production. The lighting should be chosen to light task areas and to create a pleasant working environment for the associates. Practical, easily maintained, long wearing materials should be selected for the operating departments.

The display departments should have adequate space for the design staff and be furnished with drawing tables and supply caddies. These areas should be lit with well balanced light because color selection done by the designer is critical. Storage areas must be provided for fixtures. Some fixtures are used on the selling floor at special times only and must be stored in a safe convenient location. A storage area must also be created for mannequins. Storage areas for display materials must be separated with one for large panels, one for furniture and antiques, and one for general materials and supplies. An area must be set aside for the sign machines and equipment, allowing adequate space for the production. If the store is large enough, a paint shop and a carpenter shop must be created. Storage must be provided for hardware, lumber and paint. A large working area must be provided for the staff members to build, make and modify display props and materials. Office space will be needed for the display director, assistant and secretary. □

10

Information Sources

It is inevitable for designers to get into a rut occasionally. They get involved in their own store design problems and eventually run out of ideas. Ruts can be avoided by checking the competition for new ideas. It is wise to see what other stores are doing. The ways in which they solve their presentation problems might inspire you to adapt, update, or evolve new concepts. From time to time, you should tour competing stores to see firsthand how effective their displays are. Visit specialty stores. A shoe store, for example, will have exploited most concepts about shoe presentation. Look at a grocery store to see how they impact and classify their merchandise. Visit high fashion shops for glamour ideas. Follow the windows of the best designers in town. Look for color trends and how new display materials are used. Good designers will always be more innovative with lighting, presenting merchandise, and implementing all the elements of design. The best designers spend hours poring over information looking for trends and evaluating new design concepts. (Figure 10-1)

When you go to market on the East or West Coast, check all kinds of stores out for ideas. Regions have distinctively different styles of presenting merchandise and designing displays. New York stores might be the first to establish these trends because they are close to the display manufacturers and their main showrooms. They are in the center of the fashion and apparel market, so therefore they receive and present fashion merchandise sooner than any other stores. Since the current merchandise establishes

153

10-1 Adel Rootstein, London, England

the presentation, it is inevitable that New York stores are developing ideas sooner than others. A word of caution: do not copy ideas just because they are new if they do not relate to your merchandise. Some new presentation concepts will relate to your merchandise, some will not. The most important rule is to present merchandise in an appropriate manner.

Southern stores may not be in the coat business as strongly as northern stores. Small resort stores impact active sportswear better than a metropolitan store. A department store can project a different image than can a fashion specialty store. A mass merchant will use a different philosophy about signs than another retailer. Borrow only those ideas that relate to your store.

There are many publications that can provide you with information that will help you do a better job. In addition to in-house reports, which will be discussed later in this chapter, there is a proliferation of external publications.

A. **The Shelter Magazines.** *Interiors, Interior Design, House and Garden,* and *Architectural Digest* are but a few magazines that cover news about the interior industry. They are consumer magazines, that is, they are sold to the general public. These magazines will tell you about new products, and how they are made and used. They have lots of color news, news about designers, and interviews with professionals that reveal their design philosophies. Comments from the consumer tell you about the salability of the products and reveal ideas about their use. Stories about the manufacturer tell how the product is made. Photos of the best designed rooms in the country provide information about style and taste and give you clues about good design. Your customers read these magazines at about the same time you do. They will be informed and expect you to present the new merchandise trends they have been reading about.

Trade shelter magazines are sold to and received by the people in the industry, as opposed to consumer shelter magazines. *Home Furnishings Daily* is one example. They suggest presentation ideas and detail market trends. Articles that critique retailers tell us about the hottest sellers and review the success and failures of doing business. They preview markets, alerting us to new product arrivals.

B. **Financial Newspapers.** They tell us about our important business resources. The *Wall Street Journal* is filled with news about economic trends. They critique the retail industry, giving us great insight into what we should be doing to capitalize on business. They tell us of economic indicators that influence our growth in the market and alert us to dying markets. They warn us of collapsing competitors and manufacturers, some of whom supply us.

C. **Fashion Magazines.** *Vogue, Harper's Bazaar, Mademoiselle,* and *Women's Wear Daily* provide articles, photographs, and drawings of the latest fashion trends. Interviews with designers, consumers, manufacturers, and retailers provide us with enormous information and inspiration about the merchandise. The color, design, and where and when it is to be worn is covered in depth. Accessory, makeup, and hair style trends are reviewed in these magazines. Drawings illustrate new fabrics, their patterns, color, and texture, giving us a wealth of ideas about their use and combinations. Photographs of new fashion models influence the style of mannequins we use. Backgrounds for the fashion models reveal the kind of mood we might re-create in our displays and windows. Seeing an illustration or photograph showing how the model is dressed will direct you in dressing and accessorizing mannequins. A fashion retailer must use these magazines for fashion evaluation and interpretation.

D. **Retail Magazines.** Magazines such as *Retail Week* and *Stores* are written about the retail industry in total. News coverage of personnel, merchandise, how to sell, how to buy, how to present merchandise, how to manage stores, where to locate and expand, and where to find and use capital are but a few topics written about in these magazines. Articles providing insight on how stores buy and present merchandise are an endless source for you in developing new ideas. Stories that exhaustively cover and illustrate a competitor's image provide us with ideas about our own.

E. **Display Magazines.** *Visual Merchandising* is a trade magazine geared specifically to the display business. Its photographs, drawings, and articles keep us abreast of the display business. We can read and evaluate what other stores and designers are doing on a timely basis. New sources for display materials and fixtures are brought to our attention. You might see stories on planning and how to make a display in the same issue. Interviews with designers give us insight into their creativity. Articles about window displays, store interiors, and store design are covered by this magazine.

Inspiration, another magazine for the display designer, covers pictorially the work of display designers in this country as well as abroad. The beautiful photographs help illustrate how others present merchandise. It is a source for developing ideas for windows, store design and merchandise presentation.

In addition to the magazines just listed, major department stores generate many in-house publications that can be of help to the display designer. When buyers return from market, they will submit reports at a meeting to describe their purchases. They will tell you what merchandise they have bought and from whom; how many pieces of each style they have purchased and in what sizes, color, and fabric. They will have distilled general fashion looks by the quantity of merchandise they buy. One store cannot represent or buy all of the fashion merchandise at market. One person cannot buy all the fashion looks for his department that he saw at market.

This merchandise or buyer's report is the most important guide for you.

You must create impact with that merchandise in the store, and present that merchandise in windows and displays. The object is to establish a buying mood for those goods, emphasizing their fashion news. You must create color stories around the merchandise in relationship to the quantities purchased. It is unwise to create large displays with goods that are not bought in quantity. The importance of the display must relate to the sales percentage that merchandise contributes to the total store's business. A category of merchandise that represents fifty percent of the store's total business should be emphasized with that amount of effort. You should not highlight goods that do not represent the store's strength. The buyer's commitment to purchase is the store's strength that is reflected in merchandise quantities.

The buyers will alert you to the merchandise arrivals so that your displays can be planned ahead and be timely. You certainly want to impact new arrivals instead of merchandise that has been in stock. You will find that the competition is fast to impact new arrivals and you will want to be as current with presentation as they are.

The buyers can tell you how the merchandise was presented at market, helping you decide how to present it in the store. She will tell you what manufacturers are represented in her purchases. Develop a strategy to give it identity when needed. For example, manufacturers are grouped within a shop concept or as a store's classification.

The buyers' newsletters will review a whole season of purchases, alerting you to plan its presentation in advance for every department in the store at the appropriate time. The buyers' newsletters will be modified from time to time to compensate for changes in their buying strategies.

The fashion merchandising associates will produce a report in the form of a newsletter, emphasizing the distilled fashion looks that truly represent the store's merchandising philosophy. This report will emphasize the noteworthy fashion quality of the goods bought. They are more comprehensive than individual buyer reports because they reflect the purchases of many buyers from many divisions. The fashion merchandise reports instruct when the best looks should be on what mannequins, when and how to put these fashion looks together and how to accessorize them. They should be correlated with the advertising campaigns and special events. Since the fashion merchandise associates will have been at market with the buyers, helping them select merchandise for the current fashion trends, they will have seen how the merchandise was shown, and will be sensitive to its presentation. They will give you direction on how best to present the merchandise, instruct what colors best represent the goods, and how to show the best merchandise mix.

The advertising department will produce a report on when, how and where this merchandise is to be advertised. Their reports include schedules and sketches illustrating the theme of the ad. The advertised merchandise should reflect the ad theme when it is presented. Advertised merchandise must be impacted in the store. Also, it must have current signs emphasizing the ad copy.

Company newsletters provide news about personnel and store activities to keep you and your staff informed. New shops, new resources, and new merchandise arrivals are reviewed in them. Also, company benefits, activities, and goals are spelled out.

The display department will supply reports to keep associates abreast of upcoming promotions, the use of new fixtures, signs, etc, as well as company-wide sales, promotions, and events.

The special events department will provide you with reports on guest appearances. They detail what special equipment is needed, such as sound and lighting equipment. Some craft-oriented events might need water, tools, and special tables. The need for windows and special signs announcing the event are covered in their reports. The outline of location, days, and time of the event is an important part of the report.

Magazines will help you understand the overall trends in display presentation. Company reports and newsletters distill this information, providing you with direction relating to your store.

There are times when the written material will not cover a point as graphically as a video presentation. Suppliers and manufacturers produce video tapes showing their latest couture collections. *Harper's Bazaar* and *Women's Wear Daily* sell video tapes showing the latest Paris and New York collections. Manufacturers produce tapes describing new products in detail. They explain how the product was made, who designed it, who the customer, is on what kind of fixture it is to be presented, and where the fixture is to be located in a department. The merchandise introduction time, what the ads look like, and where they will appear are points illustrated in these tapes.

With all this information available, there is no reason to run out of ideas and stay in a rut. There are countless sources of inspiration to stimulate creativity in display design. The magazines and reports will provide you with an enormous amount of reference material.

You can continually compare how you are doing in relation to other stores. You can develop presentation goals that are in tune to your store, as well as being in tune with national retail. ◻

11

The Freelance Display Designer

Many stores cannot afford a permanent display staff. Some stores are too small to employ even a display designer.

These stores will assign a sales associate to present the merchandise in the store and windows. However, this is not always a desirable situation. The taste level of these associates might not represent the store's image. The option is to hire a free lance display designer.

Free lance display designers work and schedule their time to fit the needs of a small operator. They generally are not in the employ of the store. The store might need the services of a free lance designer once a week or every two weeks to present new merchandise in the windows. They might employ the designer to arrange all the merchandise in the store once a month. Some stores will call on the designer when there are plans to expand or remodel the site. Banks, restaurants, and hotels often hire a designer to design, buy, and install their Christmas trim. Developers will hire a designer to design the interior of their shopping mall for major seasons.

Sometimes the free lance designer will be hired to consult with the retailer about his display problems. The designer will help the client arrive at his design goals, which the client will execute himself.

Exhibitions generate work for the free lance designer. Exhibits must be designed and installed. Manufacturers who are in St. Louis must find a local Chicago designer to help present their merchandise when they are showing

11-1 Wally Findlay Galleries, Chicago IL

there. Museums will recruit the help of a display designer for designing and installing special exhibits. (Figure 11-1) Fashion and social groups will hire a designer to help produce a special fashion show or help decorate a restaurant for a special luncheon. Small towns will hire the services of a display designer to help them choose Christmas decorations for the main street.

A free lance designer is selling his design ability. A fee should be charged for the project based on time spent, by the hour, directly to the client. A contract should be written spelling out work to be covered. This eliminates billing disputes.

It is important to set up an office. An office can be set up in the designer's house to reduce costs or else space can be rented. Good accounting procedures should be established to account for costs and for proper billing. If you hire help, this requires special accounting. This is all needed by law for tax purposes.

Some designers have small studios or workshops where they can produce art, make signs, or make displays. If you do not have studio space, all materials needed for your display should be purchased and sent in advance to the store and billed to that store. All displays should be fabricated at a display manufacturer and drop shipped to the store. The store should understand this plan so receivables are properly handled and paid for.

A free lance designer must arrive with all the tools and display materials needed for the job. This requires advanced planning. The lack of staff and the need for portability of his equipment will not allow elaborate productions, similar to a store with a permanent staff and shop. Some stores want a simple effective arrangement of their merchandise in the windows. Recovering pads with fresh material, placing a sign, and adding a floral arrangement might be the only requirement. Some designers are asked only to change mannequins in the window or rig men's forms in a store for men.

Before you accept the job, you might advise that the store remodel their windows to add better lighting and more effective space to handle simple merchandise presentation.

It is important for the designer to evaluate the store's image quickly and to evaluate the fashion philosophy. A return trip might be necessary after first consultation to more effectively discuss the work needed. Bill the client for preliminary ideas and consulting. Time spent arriving at the contract should not be billed.

The store manager must have the merchandise selected and ready for your arrival, unless as part of the job he wants your help with the merchandise selection.

On occasion, the display job might need special installations and custom work done by subcontractors. There are display studios that can execute the display and install it for you. Your job is to supervise special installations and provide art direction. This is especially true with bank and plaza

Christmas installations. The designer does not have the tools, space, equipment, or staff to handle such large jobs.

The discipline of promptness, reliability and proper timing is essential. You must learn to pace your work evenly. Try not to take on too much until you are equipped for it. The quantity of work will grow with your reputation. Referrals come to you through word of mouth.

Many fully employed junior designers are involved in free lance work to supplement their salaries. They generally schedule work for weekends and a few nights. The work schedule should not interfere with your full time employment.

The free lance designer will need a supply of staple guns, tacks, scissors, wire pliers, hammers, saws, all of which should be portable. The preparation of display props must be partially done in advance. The tools should be needed for installation only, or for small modifications of the display materials. You cannot expect to turn a client's store into a workshop, and besides, there is probably little extra space for this. Most stores do not have surplus storage space, so all material must be transported to and from location. It is a priority that the designer own a van or station wagon to provide mobility and to move his display materials to the location.

Display suppliers and jobbers are a good source for generating new clients. They sell material to retailers, but are not interested in doing display work. Display jobbers are often asked to recommend designers. Some have in-house designers to do store diplays, and as their work load increases, they need to supplement their staff with free lancers.

Department stores need the help of free lancers from time to time. They are hired for additional help with Christmas installations and for events that cannot be handled by the store's display staff. The designer must develop prompt, professional billing procedures, because the clients want to be billed in the month that the work had been budgeted for.

Junior colleges and high schools provide adult education courses that cover basic accounting and business procedures. They are a must for the designer. The government small business bureau can consult with you, provide reading material that will assist you in acquiring this knowledge.

Free lance designers may specialize in high fashion or mass merchandising, ranging from shoe stores to men's clothing stores.

Some free lance display designers travel from city to city to consult with management teams about their image and presentation problems.

The free lance designer must read enormous amounts of materials to keep abreast of trends. He does not have the help that staff designers have from their merchandising associates in providing merchandise information. He must visit display markets to keep current on the newest display materials and fixtures. This is all part of doing business for yourself, but the development of fashion awareness will be most rewarding. □

12

The Grid

As a guide in presenting merchandise or arranging fixtures, it is helpful to think of an imaginary grid. The grid will help you arrange the merchandise in a clear, orderly manner. The following drawings illustrate the merchandise in the form of basic geometric symbols and patterns — the square, rectangle, triangle, and circle. You can elaborate on the grid and geometric system by making complex geometric form combinations of a basic triangle, rectangle, square, or circle.

Figure 12-1

This illustration shows the appropriate way to present merchandise in a showcase with either an open or closed front. Begin by grouping the merchandise within a class, such as cosmetics, purses, or small leather goods. The case must house only one class. Beginning at the left, work from top to bottom, arranging similar items in neat rows. Try not to overcrowd. Imagine a grid superimposed over the front of the case as a guide. Continue to arrange all the merchandise in vertical rows until complete. If there are many cases for a class, try to arrange the merchandise by the size of the product. Group small items together, likewise with medium and large. If the product has a wide range of color, think of the color wheel or spectrum. Begin with the violet to blue family on the left, followed by the green family, the red family, and the yellow family. The neutrals will be split — the dark neutrals should precede violet and the light neutrals should follow yellow.

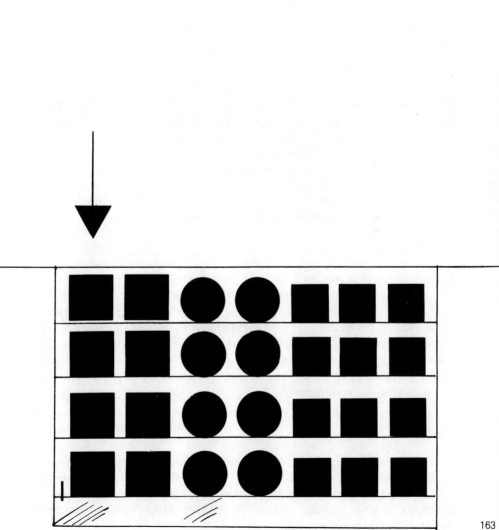

Figure 12-2

This illustration shows the top of a case, viewed from above. Here again, use your imaginary grid. Arrange the merchandise from front to rear in neat rows, with large items on the left to smaller items on the right. You might prefer to arrange the merchandise in reverse, with large items starting from the right. The important thing is to be consistent. Be sure that your arrangement relates to the design of the fixture and the merchandise you stock. The illustrated grid and symbols could represent the arrangement of jewelry, bracelets, cosmetics, china, wine, or hair pieces.

Figure 12-3

Grocers arrange their stock from left to right in a grid. However, they prefer a horizontal pattern because of their large fixtures and extremely long rows of shelving with many shelves per row. Each item is placed only as far right or left as not to exceed the customers' scope of vision. They will arrange items horizontally — smaller items at the top, larger items at the bottom. They also arrange merchandise within a class — all coffee together, all sugar together. They take into consideration the popularity of the item when making the arrangement.

Figure 12-4

If the showcase has a back wall, make sure that the merchandise in the up-front case continues to that back wall. This keeps all similar merchandise well within the customers' vision. Work with the grid system and the color principles in arranging the package or product. Keep the class together, and the assortment of items in neat rows.

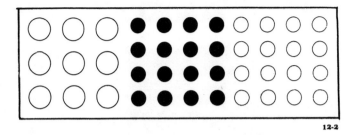

12-2

12-3

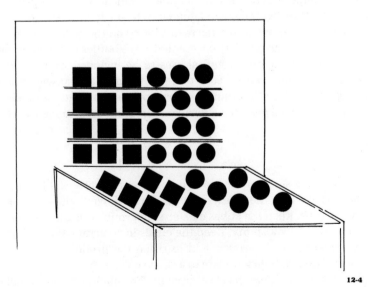

12-4

Figure 12-5

When arranging merchandise on a cube or tabletop, use the grid system. Work from left to right, dark to light, large to small, in rows front to back. Other modified geometric arrangements based on the grid can be used. For example, if this arrangement represented were bottles of wine, modify the grid to allow a sample tray and glasses to be included. Foods and wines adapt to this system well. Be sure that you arrange all red wine and white separately, but within the country of origin. There are endless qualities of a product that will suggest or inspire you about an arrangement.

Figure 12-6

When arranging stock on several cubes that are at different heights, place the shortest stock on the tallest cube, grading it down to the tallest items on the lowest cube. Keep the cubes clustered in groups using a grid concept — single cubes can look spotty. Keep the cubes in an arrangement that allows the customers to walk around and to reach the product with ease. Class and color arrangement can relate to a single cube, or you can use the group of three cubes to project the class or color. The amount of stock will dicate how it is broken down for the arrangement.

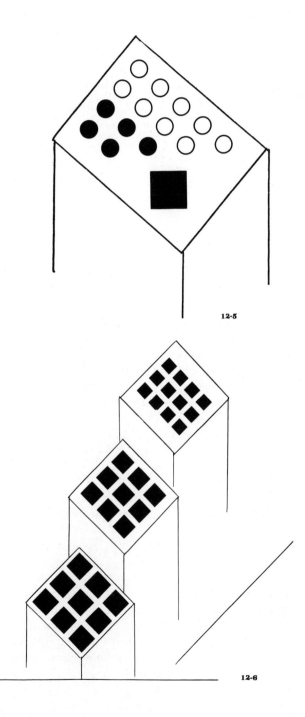

12-5

12-6

Figure 12-7

If the assortment of merchandise is in small quantities and you are working with a cube cluster, each item may be arranged within item color and size on each cube. The grid concept will help your create order in your presentation and also help the sales associate be aware when stocks are low. At a glance, she will be able to tell how many items are remaining in her stock. This is hard to do when merchandise is placed helter skelter all over the department. The self service customer can also locate merchandise easier when presented this way.

Figure 12-8

Keep the lower, smaller fixtures forward, the taller, larger fixtures back. Do not arrange the cubes or fixtures so they visually block each other. Tall apparel fixtures should be at the back of the department and the short ones up front at the carpet line.

Figure 12-9

Arrange all the cubes and fixtures on the floor on an imaginary grid pattern, creating straight aisles and sight lines from side to side and front to back. Arrange smaller fixtures up front and larger ones to the back. Small display cubes can be at the carpet line up front for displays and special presentation. Arrange the clusters of fixtures and cubes in the same grid concept that dictated the overall floor arrangement.

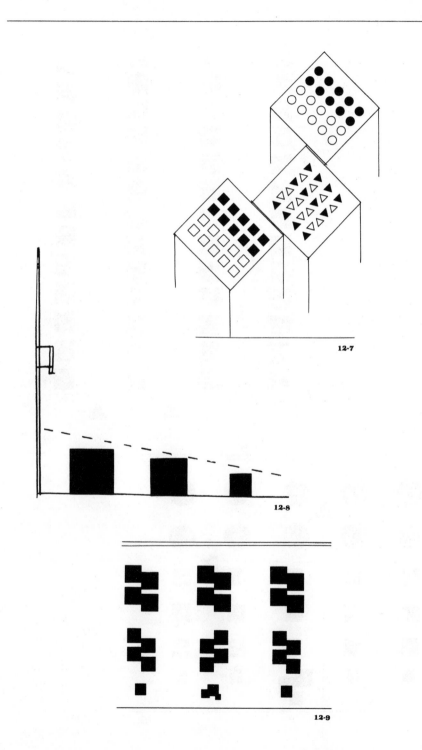

12-7

12-8

12-9

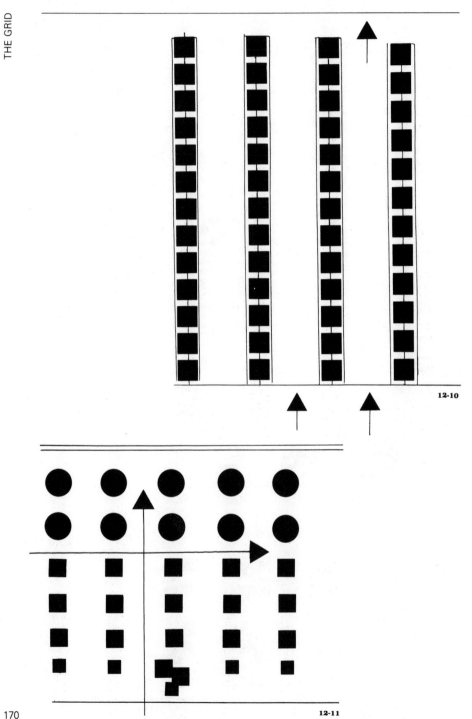

12-10

12-11

Figure 12-10

If you use long rows of connecting fixtures for foods, hardware, automotive parts, or housewares items, arrange the rows so that they run from the front to the back of the department. This plant creates good traffic aisles, allowing the customers to walk to the back wall to select other categories of merchandise. If the fixtures are arranged in the opposite direction, they will create a barricade, making it difficult for customers to walk through the total department. The merchandise housed in the back wall might not be the correct size for the free standing fixtures or the back wall could be an area to impact special merchandise.

Figure 12-11

Arrange apparel fixtures so that the largest fixture (round racks) are at the rear of the department. These fixtures will house large quantities of merchandise. The large rounders should house merchandise that is also hung on the back wall. Arrange smaller fixtures (four arms or quads) in front of the rounders. These fixtures will hold smaller coordinate groups. They will allow you to break your merchandise into groups of color, fabrication, silhouette, style, highlight, or any special way your stock dictates. Place smaller fixtures (T-stands or costumers) up front. The T-stands will allow you to feature ad merchandise, or hang a special fashion look from the quads. Place mannequins on cubes at the front of the department. The adjacent T-stands and quad fixtures should house the merchandise shown on the mannequins. Arrange all of the fixtures on an imaginary grid in neat rows from front to back and side to side. This arrangement will allow customers to clearly see the entire department and walk through it with ease. It will help you organize the groups of merchandise on the floor. A clear, orderly look is established, thereby eliminating crowded, unorganized looks.

171

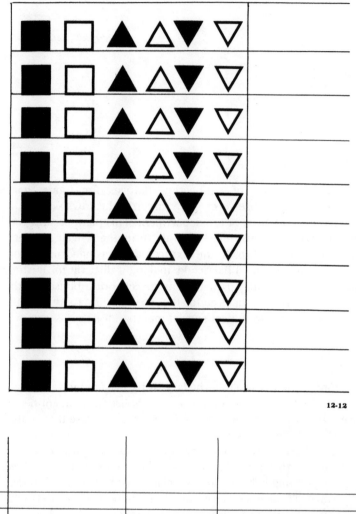

12-12

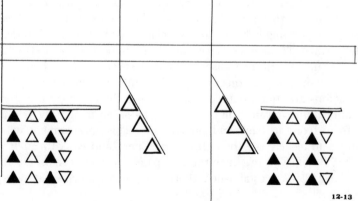

12-13

Figure 12-12

Merchandise on shelves on a back wall should be arranged vertically. This keeps each style of merchandise within the customers' normal vision. Start at the top, arranging each piece from top to bottom in neat rows, work from left to right creating rows of color, dark to light and sizes, large to small. A class of merchandise can be arranged together within each module of shelving. Always allow some feature of the merchandise to influence your arrangement.

Figure 12-13

Use the imaginary grid to arrange the back wall merchandise. Break up the arrangement by adding shelves or waterfall face-out arms with apparel rods. The face-out arms will allow the customer to see the front of the garment or item. Long rows of either shelves or apparel rods will create an overcrowded, monotonous look. The back wall mixed fixture arrangement will allow you to break up long runs of merchandise into groups of color, fashion, style, fabrication, and silhouette. If you highlight designer name merchandise, you can group those designers more effectively. Keep color groups together. The face-out bars should house adjacent merchandise hung on apparel rods or folded on shelves. □

13

Racks and Displayers

Figure 13-1

Rows of T-shirts hanging on apparel dress rods look better if the rows are broken up by waterfall face-out bars. This arrangement lets you show the fronts of the shirts on the bars and house quantities of them on the rods. The shirts on the face-out bars should be identical to the shirts hanging on the rods, that is, they should have the same sleeve lengths, silhouette, and style. Be sure to arrange shirts of the same color together. For example, all red shirts create a red statement. If you cannot make this statement because of limited quantities of stock, you can arrange the shirts on the rod from left to right in accordance with the color spectrum.

Figure 13-2

Hang all apparel on round racks within groups having the same color, fabrication, style, and silhouette. All hem and sleeve lengths should be the same. If you have several groups on one rounder, try to establish a pattern so there is an even progression from one group to another. You will probably have more than one rounder to work with, so hang all similar merchandise together. You will find you can hang all sleeveless apparel within order on one rounder and all sleeved merchandise within order on another. Remember, clutter exists if you mix up the styles.

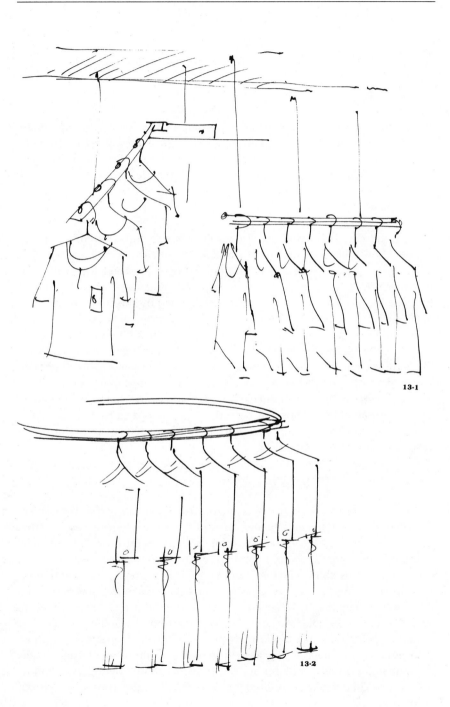

13-1

13-2

Figure 13-3

If you group all sleeveless dresses in the same style, color, and hem length together, you create an organized look. This makes it easier for the customers to make merchandise selections, sales associates to locate styles and the merchandise manager to determine stock levels.

Figure 13-4

Arrange all patterned merchandise within color groups. All florals, for example, should be grouped using the color spectrum or color wheel as a guide. Show all red floral on one rounder, all yellow geometrics on another. If the merchandise levels will not allow this arrangement, then arrange all florals within color groups in progression guided by the color spectrum — violet to blue to green to yellow to red. This color sequence is observed in a rainbow or when a beam of white light passes through a glass prism.

You might prefer to develop your own color arrangement. I like to use black to blue to green to red to yellow to white. This arrangement enables you to develop a sequence of dark colors to the lightest ones. It also allows you to arrange a better sequence of overlapping colors, black to red-blue to blue to green-blue to blue-red to red to yellow-red to yellow to green-yellow. Experiment with the colors to determine a sequence that best corresponds to your merchandise.

Figure 13-5

A mix of colors and patterns is a confusing arrangement that causes customers to take too much time to find a desired item. Because of the movement toward self selection, it is imperative that the customers must be able to locate color, style, and patterns as quickly and easily as possible. A hodgepodge is established when you begin to mix merchandise on a fixture. A red dress hanging next to a green dress may make the colors of both dresses look bad. If a customer finds a desirable red dress, she may have to sort through many color variations before she finds one in or her size. The matching red dress may be on the other side of the rounder. Mixing patterns is not a good idea — a floral pattern does not complement a geometric. Also, mixing fabrics is a bad practice. All wools should be together and all linens should be together. A linen will look frail hanging next to a textured woolen fabric.

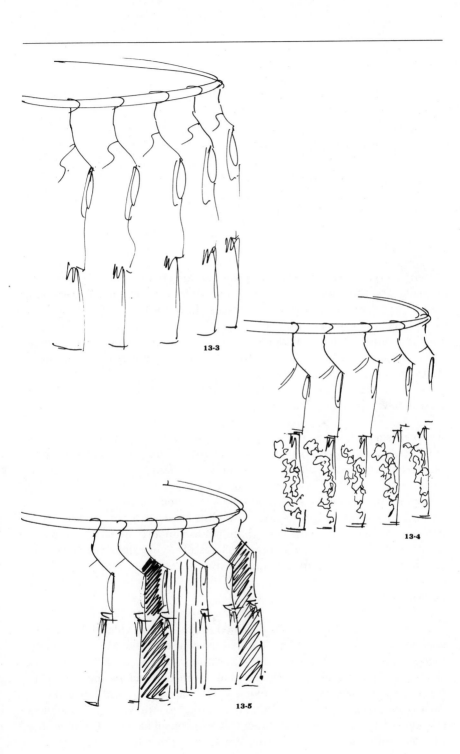

13-3

13-4

13-5

Figure 13-6

When you hang all the same styles together, you create a neat, well organized look. The repetition of the style makes stronger statements, creating a
better product impact. Repeated items also have the effect of making your
stock look complete. However, be careful in your zeal to present merchandise that you do not overcrowd fixtures. Customers find it difficult to
remove apparel from jammed fixtures. Also, keep in mind that showing
items in quantity does not always sell the items.

Figure 13-7

A mix of sleeve lengths, hem lengths, and styles hanging together side by
side on a rounder presents a choppy, confused look. The fashion image is
blurred. It will be difficult for the customers to identify the importance of a
sleeveless, full sleeve, or three-quarter sleeve dress. The mixture also
presents a disturbing message about style and hem lengths. If your store's
collection is small and you cannot establish color, style, or fabrication in
depth, you should not hang your merchandise on a rounder. A rounder is
for large quantities of merchandise. Perhaps all of your store's merchandise
should be hung on T-stands or quad fixtures.

Figure 13-8

The quad or four-arm fixture is designed to house small collections of merchandise. Tops such as shirts, blouses, and jackets should face forward
toward the front of the department. Bottoms such as pants, shorts, and
skirts should be hanging on the bars behind their matching tops. Hang all
tops together, matching their colors, styles, silhouettes, and fabrications.
An adjacent rounder can be used to hang large quantities of the same merchandise. A quad can be used effectively to hang all blouses. The quad fixture lets you segregate and feature any merchandise from large stocks.

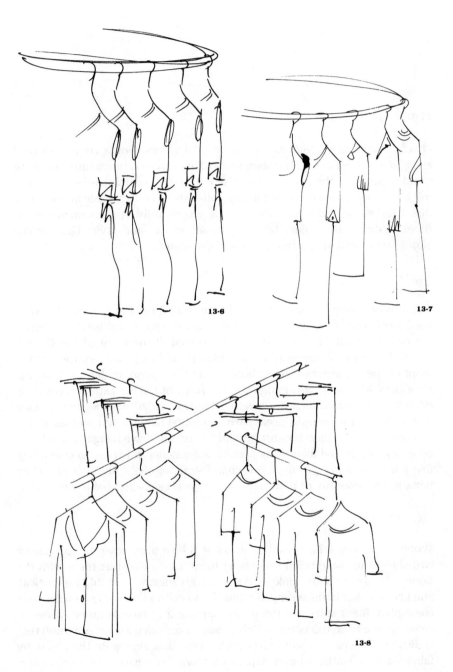

13-6

13-7

13-8

Figure 13-9

Quad fixtures are designed with four straight arms or a combination of straight and slant arms. The slant arms allow you to arrange tops in a more visible manner at the front of the fixture. The downward slanting arms permit customers to see immediately the collar styles of each piece of merchandise hanging on the arms. Arrange the merchandise groups on these fixtures within class, color, fabrication, silhouette, and style. Quad racks should be placed at the front of the department.

Figure 13-10

T-stands or costumers are best used to present a fashion statement, advertised merchandise, a color story, or to show the merchandise that is on an adjacent mannequin. The T-stands are placed at the front of the department. Hang tops on the slant bars, which should be positioned toward the front of the department. Hang bottoms on the horizontal bars behind the slant bars. The top that is hanging at the front of the bar can be accessorized. If the tops are jackets, you can tuck blouses under them. Since you hang so few items on T-stands, great care should be taken when you select the merchandise. The merchandise should be current, have hangar appeal, and be easily recognized as making specific statements. It is easy to take a few items from a larger group of merchandise to highlight on T-stands. Then hang larger amounts of merchandise on quad racks just behind them.

Figure 13-11

When presenting a back wall of shirts, it is best to remove the top one or two shelves to make room for a shirt form. Dress the shirt form with the same color as the shirts below. The color arrangement should be vertical. Shirt colors should be arranged from left to right in accordance with your color plan. Black shirts on the top, progressing to blue to green to red to yellow to white on the bottom. This creates a conspicuous presentation that allows customers to select shirts with ease. Also, segregate the shirts by fabrication — waffle weaves separated from flat weaves. The shirt form shows the shirt body and its detailing.

13-9

13-10

13-11

Figure 13-12

You can make back walls more interesting by rearranging long rows of shelves or hang rods. Neat rows of shelves can be topped with apparel forms. This adds interest to the merchandise and makes it more visible. Variety can be added with the addition of hang rods and face-out bars. By arranging the merchandise in small groups, you reduce the merchandise to a more human scale. Great amounts of merchandise can overwhelm customers. A wall of shirt shelves can be monotonous. If the wall is 25 feet long, the scale of one shirt is insignificant when compared to the entire wall of shirts. The shirt is more significant when it is seen in relationship to a smaller groups of shirts. Rearrangement of the shelves plus the addition of hang bars and shirt forms makes it easier to develop color, fabric, and style groups.

Figure 13-13

A mannequin at the front of a department strengthens your presentation, especially when placed on a platform. Choose a mannequin that best fits the look of the department. Its age, posture, make up, and hair style should be in keeping with the merchandise. The illustration shows a seated mannequin dressed in sportswear. The mannequin could just as easily have been seated on a wicker trunk or packing crate instead of the platform cube. Accessories should be carefully selected. The scarf, shoes, and jewelry should further develop the sportswear look. Merchandise similar to that on the mannequin should be hanging on a T-stand immediately behind or to one side. More of the same merchandise can be placed on a quad rack behind the T-stand. Because of the mannequin's impact on the customers, you should dress it in the best manner possible.

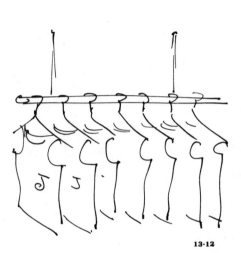

13-12

13-13

Figure 13-14

Two mannequins let you present more merchandise. You can clothe both in dresses of the same style, thus repeating and strengthening your statement. Or you can clothe the mannequins in dresses having similar styles. This has the effect of making both dresses look more important. Customers can view as many as two or three mannequins at the same time without being distracted. Accessories for the mannequins should be of the same class, design, color, and price. Again, the same clothing styles that the mannequins are wearing should be hanging on adjacent T-stands and quad fixtures for the customers' inspection.

Figure 13-15

Housewares and gift objects are best arranged on back wall shelves in neat rows from top to bottom. Try to find a feature that all the merchandise has in common and let that guide you in deciding what items are to be placed next to one another. For example, all the items might be made of pottery, painted the same colors, and designed for the same life styles. Arrange the merchandise until you have developed an obvious theme. Arrange another category on the next shelf module, using the same method, and continue in this manner until you have presented the entire collection. If they are attractive, large boxed items can be shown on the lower shelves below the unboxed items.

13-14

13-15

Figure 13-16

Advertised items are highly visible to customers when you take some of the items from stock and place them on a platform located in an aisle at the front of a department, or in an aisle at the end of a row of fixtures. A sign placed next to the presentation identifies the advertised items and reinforces the sale's message. This arrangement is most effective when you present only one product on the platform. For customer convenience, back-up stock should be close at hand. Keep in mind that customers become very frustrated and irritated when they cannot find advertised items in a department.

Figure 13-17

At special times of the year such as Easter, Mothers' Day, Fathers' Day, Valentine's Day, St. Patrick's Day, and Christmas, it is a good practice to pre-wrap gift items. Choose a table size that matches the scale of the merchandise to be pre-wrapped, and place the table in a traffic area at the front of a department. Select a cloth cover for the table that complements the gift wrapping paper and, if possible, the colors of the season. Place only one type of gift on each table. This avoids the possibility of customers becoming confused with a helter skelter arrangement of many gifts. Some of the items on the table should not be wrapped to permit customer inspections. Place a sign on the table that describes the gift merchandise. Stock additional gift merchandise on an adjacent fixture. Pre-wraps help sell merchandise and they contribute to the decorative appearance of the department. □

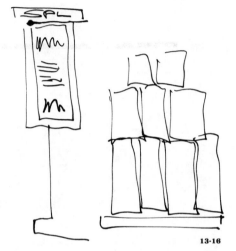

13-16

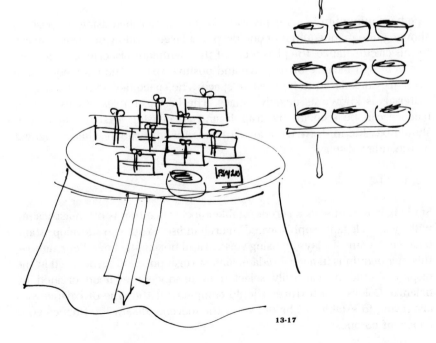

13-17

14

Display
Composition

Figure 14-1

The bare minimum in art expression for visual merchandising purposes is showing one mannequin and one prop in a large window or display space. In this circumstance, the placement of the mannequin is critical. The solution is design balance of negative and positive space. The mannequin and prop are considered to be positive space. The space devoid of any display materials is known as negative space. The best examples of this kind of balance can be seen in the graphic and advertising arts. However, you should be able to draw from all art forms for inspiration when designing merchandise displays.

Figure 14-2

Static balance conveys a serene, stable appearance that is often associated with very elegant sophisticated merchandise. You can develop static balance in your displays by using vertical and horizontal lines. For example, this mannequin is in a very sedate, almost regal pose. All forms used in the display should be carefully selected to produce the mood created by balance. Colors and textures should complement the type of balance you are trying to establish. The design of the merchandise will influence your choice of composition.

14-1

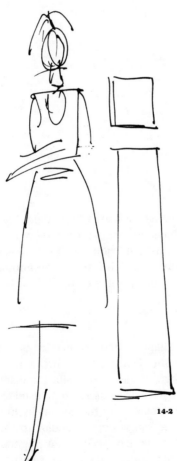

14-2

Figure 14-3

The active look is developed by lines at an angle. Mannequins and props placed at an angle or having angled lines create a dynamic appearance. Sportive merchandise lends itself quite well to the active look, which the bright colors further enhance. Use simple thumbnail sketches to help organize your thoughts about display composition.

Figure 14-4A, Figure 14-4B

Use the basic geometric shapes — the circle, triangle, square, and rectangle — to help you design your display. A circle can be used to develop the display floor plan. Arrange all the elements of the display in a circle on the floor, as in illustration A. The circle can also be used to develop the display elevation. Arrange all the elements of the display including the mannequins so that they form a circle that is perpendicular to the floor in the visual plane, as in illustration B. You can accentuate the circle by using apparel fabrics with circular designs and prop with circular patterns in the display.

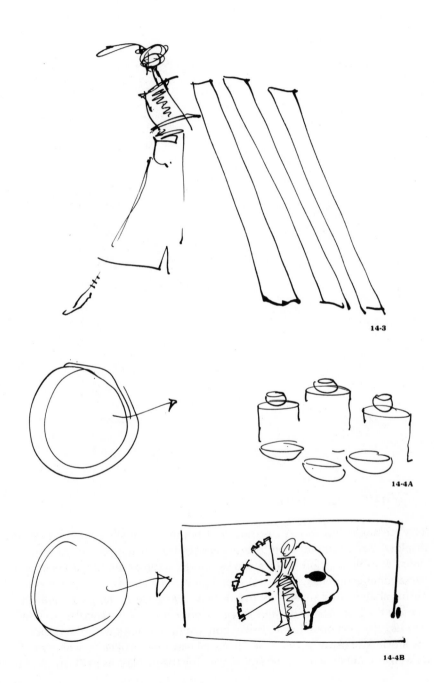

14-3

14-4A

14-4B

Figure 14-5A, Figure 14-5B

The rectangle and square are the most popular geometric shapes used in displays. For example, furniture is arranged in rectangles on the display floor, as in illustration A. This allows you to arrange the furniture in conversational groupings. Also, the rectangles and squares are the basic furniture shapes, and most window display areas are rectangular. For that matter, the basic shape of most stores' architecture is rectangular, so when you use the rectangle for a display you are in harmony with the design of the store. The use of a rectangle for visual elevation evokes a specific mood, as well as complementing the space used for the display, as in illustration B.

14-5A

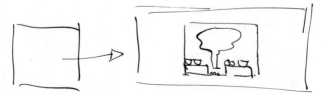

14-5B

Figure 14-6A, Figure 14-6B, Figure 14-6C

The triangle can be an active element in a display, as in illustration A. The two acute angles in the right triangle in the visual elevation convey a feeling of action. Conversely, an equilateral triangle makes for a very sedate, stable display, as in illustration B. This is because the equal sides and equal angles place all the items in the display in geometric balance. The use of geometric shapes as starting points for your displays might seem quite academic, but you have to start someplace and these shapes give you a good basis on which you can elaborate. Also, consideration of the basic design principles will help you develop display ideas without being bogged down by too many details. Try to reduce your conceptual design ideas to simple statements. The beginning of a display can be a small sketch that can guide you through the complex activity of completing your display. Illustration C shows a triangle being used to develop the arrangement of mannequins and props on a display floor plan.

14-6A

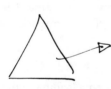

14-6B

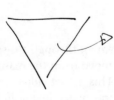

14-6C

Figure 14-7

A half circle can be effectively used to develop a display floor plan or visual elevation, as in illustration 7. Endless design variations can be created with the basic geometric shapes. These shapes are old composition tools but the merchandise and props will always be new and interesting. Each season there are new colors, textures, designs, and fashions to work with.

Figure 14-8

Placing articles of merchandise on the floor in a row leading to the rear of a display carries the customers' eyes to the rear of the display. You can carry the customers' line of sight to any location in the display by changing the angle of the row of merchandise. To add variety, you can alter the size of the merchandise. However, be careful not to use articles of merchandise that vary so greatly in size that they interrupt the visual sight line.

Figure 14-9

Customers' eyes move from element to element through a display from the front to the rear. In the illustration, eyes move from the mannequin to the backdrop, and then up the backdrop. This effect adds height to your display. If the display is cluttered with too many items, it is difficult to establish any line of sight.

14-7

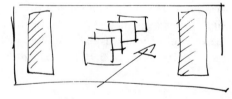

14-8

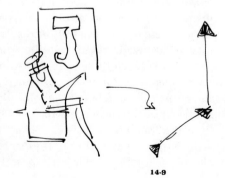

14-9

Figure 14-10

The customers' eyes travel around the circle from mannequin to mannequin in illustration A. The floor plan for this display is shown in illustration
B. Illustration C shows a geometric analysis of the composition. It is a good
plan to make sketches of your displays, showing them as geometric solids.
These sketches will help you to better visualize dimensional displays.

Figure 14-11

Lighting diagrams help you plan the lighting you are going to use in display
windows. Proper lightings achieves the following: makes your displays
sparkle; highlights the colors of the merchandise; controls your composition; and makes the customers concentrate on the areas of the display that
are highlighted. Ceiling spotlights of 300 watts positioned above and in
front of a sofa will highlight it, as in A. Because these spots are so bright,
they will eliminate most shadows. Spotlights of 250 watts positioned above
and to the front of the display, and to the right and left of the sofa, add light
and eliminate shadows that might occur at the focal edges of the 300 watt
spots, as in B. Spotlights at C are placed behind the sofa to illuminate the
back wall. This further enhances the 3-dimensional effect of the display and
gives the furniture a solid look. The light in the table lamp at D is a
decorative light source.

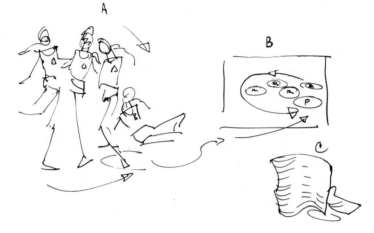

14-10

14-11

Figure 14-12

The lighting plan in this illustration is for lighting a window display that features three mannequins. The lights at A are 300 watt spotlights. They are located at the top of the display and are forward at the proscenium line. They light the mannequin faces and produce a daylight type effect. These lights are bright enough to wash out any shadows on the mannequins. The spotlights at the top left are colored to emphasize the color of the merchandise. Use the filters that best flatter the colors of the merchandise. Proscenium spotlights in B to the left and right at the top are 250 watts. They add fill-in light, washing out shadows created by the 300 watt spots. The sidelights at A are 300 watts. They balance the top lighting, eliminate shadows caused by the strong downlight, and are used to highlight features of the merchandise. The spotlights at B are 250 watts and they add fill-in light to eliminate side shadows and enhance the overall side illumination. The spots on the floor at B are 250 watts. They provide up-lighting to balance the overall light and to eliminate shadows created by the strong downlight. Because more illumination from the top proscenium dominates, you create the appearance that the display is lighted from only one source. It is important that the light is so balanced. It takes all the light sources to balance the light and to eliminate the shadows and to create the illusion of one light source. □

Index